Ethan Marcotte

RESPONSIVE DESIGN: PATTERNS AND PRINCIPLES

Publisher: Jeffrey Zeldman
Designer: Jason Santa Maria
Executive Director: Katel LeDû
Editor: Erin Kissane
Technical Editor: Anna Debenham
Copyeditor: Nicole Fenton
Proofreader: Lisa Maria Martin
Compositor: Rob Weychert
Ebook Producer: Ron Bilodeau

ISBN: 978-1-9375573-3-1

A Book Apart
New York, New York
http://abookapart.com

10 9 8 7 6 5 4 3 2 1

TABLE OF CONTENTS

1 | CHAPTER 1
Starting Small

16 | CHAPTER 2
Navigation

57 | CHAPTER 3
Images and Videos

91 | CHAPTER 4
Responsive Advertising

113 | CHAPTER 5
Designing the Infinite Grid

149 | *Resources*

151 | *Acknowledgements*

152 | *References*

158 | *Index*

FOREWORD

ETHAN MARCOTTE DIDN'T INVENT responsive web design. He did something much more important: he *named* it. He observed what was, at the time, a sprawling set of nascent tactics and identified among them an underlying strategy which, once named, became not just a way of doing web design, but *the* way of doing it. In the intervening years, the phrase "responsive web design" has become one of the few entries in the industry lexicon to find widespread adoption beyond the field, demonstrating not only the soundness of the methods but also the clarity and persuasiveness of the phrase. I was speaking to a carpenter recently when he confessed—unbidden—that it was important to him that his website be responsive.

That's the power of a great name.

Here Marcotte turns to words again, but this time to slay one: the page is dead. It was terminal the moment the first website came online, of course, but it's been a long, slow decline, marked by many moments in which it seemed to have rallied. As recently as five years ago, when *Responsive Web Design* was first published, designing web "pages" was understood to be core to the job. Since then, a deceptively subtle transformation has occurred: we've abandoned pages for modular components, ditching that dusty metaphor from print days for an organizational system much more attuned to the shifty world of the screen. Like those before, this transformation requires that we evolve both our technical approach *and* our mental model for designing experiences on the web—that is, both the code and the language we use to talk about it.

Marcotte has you covered on both fronts. As with *Responsive Web Design,* this book describes a series of smart and efficient technical strategies that you can put to work right away. (And you'd best do so quickly.) But it also suggests a compelling conceptual framework for thinking about a more modular web, leaving the page behind for good. With millions of devices and an impossible number of screens, it's about time.

—Mandy Brown

1

STARTING SMALL

" My anxiety doesn't come from thinking about the
future, but from wanting to control it. "
—HUGH PRATHER, Notes to Myself: My Struggle to Become a Person

THERE'S A TREE I want to show you.

This tree's located in Pando, which you'll find in Utah's
Fishlake National Forest in the western United States (FIG 1.1).
(It's a mile or two south of Fish Lake, if you know the area.)
And as you walk through Pando, searching for our tree, you'll
pass hundreds of stunningly beautiful aspens, their white bark
smooth to the touch, their tops covered in puffs of gold in the
autumn, or a deep, rich green in the warmer months. As lovely
as these trees are, it'll probably take you only an hour or two
of wandering to wonder where this "special" tree is, and how
it could possibly be more special than the thousands of other
trees in Pando.

Here's the thing, though: I've misled you, if only a little.
Pando's not a forest: it's a tree. More specifically, it's a single
quaking aspen.

FIG 1.1: Welcome to Pando, where we're looking for a very special tree. Photograph by J. Zapell (http://bkaprt.com/rdpp/01-01/).

You see, *pando* is the Latin word for "I spread." More scientifically, it's known as a *clonal colony:* the "trees" around us are really just stems, each sprouting up out of one massive underground root system they all share. All told, Pando weighs some six million kilograms, and covers more than one hundred acres. Its age is a topic of some debate—the National Park Service suggests Pando's been around for over 80,000 years (http://bkaprt.com/rdpp/01-02/), while some scientists put its age closer to one million years (http://bkaprt.com/rdpp/01-03/)—but there's no question that Pando is one of the largest, heaviest, and oldest known organisms on Earth.

...this is, I promise, a book about responsive design.

I love this story not just because of its details, but because in recent years, we've started to see web design's forest for its trees. With the explosion of mobile computing, we realized that our desktop-centric view of the web was entirely too narrow.

Our smaller screens reminded us that the web is the first truly *fluid* design medium: one that can be digested on nearly infinite combinations of browsers, display resolutions, input types, and device classes. Responsive design—fluid grids, flexible images, and media queries working in concert—can shape the web's flexibility in useful, beautiful ways.

Some time ago, Paravel's Trent Walton described his process of coming around to responsive design: how he'd transitioned from eyeing flexible layouts with skepticism to designing some of the loveliest responsive sites on the web. In his essay, he relates that transition beautifully(http://bkaprt.com/rdpp/01-04/):

> *I traded the control I had in Photoshop for a new kind of control—using flexible grids, flexible images, and media queries to build not a page, but a network of content that can be rearranged at any screen size to best convey a message.*

You'll probably notice that Trent says "a *new* kind of control," not "less control," which I love. He suggests that the flexibility inherent in responsive design—or heck, the flexibility at the heart of the web—doesn't mean you have to sacrifice control, aesthetics, or narrative. And the last few years have proven that point handily: from nonprofits to publishers and corporations to governments, the web has seen an explosion of stunning responsive sites, accessible to people no matter how small (or large) their screens might be (**FIG 1.2-1.5**).

As responsive design proliferates, Trent's idea of "networks of content" is more relevant than ever. In fact, the idea of a "page," that wonderful word we borrowed from print, is increasingly irrelevant to our work. I'd argue that we're no longer building pages at all—instead, we need to think of our responsive designs as a network of *small layout systems* (**FIG 1.6**). Little pockets of design that can, as Trent says, "be rearranged at any screen size to best convey a message."

Here's a quick example: open Google's Year in Search 2014 (http://bkaprt.com/rdpp/01-14/) in a resizable browser (**FIG 1.7**).

FIG 1.2: The Field Museum (http://bkaprt.com/rdpp/01-05/) and the National Audubon Society (http://bkaprt.com/rdpp/01-06/) are stunning examples of well-designed responsive nonprofit sites.

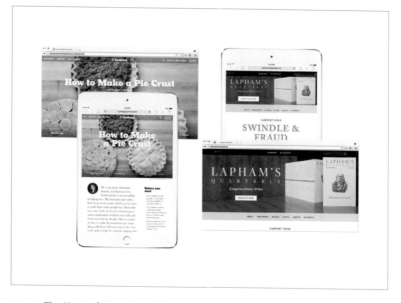

FIG 1.3: The *New York Times* (http://bkaprt.com/rdpp/01-07/) and Lapham's Quarterly (http://bkaprt.com/rdpp/01-08/) are among the many publishers going responsive.

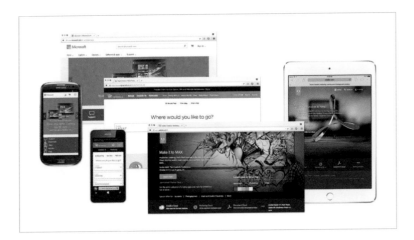

FIG 1.4: Microsoft (http://bkaprt.com/rdpp/01-09/), Virgin America (http://bkaprt.com/rdpp/01-10/), and Adobe (http://bkaprt.com/rdpp/01-11/) are a few well-known brands that have tossed their hat in the responsive ring.

FIG 1.5: Government websites are investing in responsive in a big way, including AIDS.gov, the GOV.UK (http://bkaprt.com/rdpp/01-12/), and the US Digital Service (http://bkaprt.com/rdpp/01-13/).

FIG 1.6: Beyond pages: our interfaces are composed of tiny components, or small layout systems.

FIG 1.7: Google's Year in Search 2014 is a wonderful example of self-contained responsive modules, each adapting according to its needs (http://bkaprt.com/rdpp/01-14/).

Change the size of the window, making the responsive design wide, then small, and then back again. As you resize your browser, you'll notice that the entire design reshapes itself, its fluid, grid-based layout working with media queries to respond to the changing shape of its viewport. It's a well-built piece of responsive design, to say the least.

After you resize things a few times, you'll notice not everything changes at once: the design of lead stories remains relatively unchanged, while secondary stories switch between one- and two-column layouts (FIG 1.8–9). And the navigation at the top of the screen undergoes a number of changes, each independent of the content below it (FIG 1.10). In other words, the individual components of the design change, not just the overall layout. This is true of most responsive layouts: our interfaces are composed of small layout systems, each with its own rules for how it should change, shift, and grow according to the needs of the content inside it. While these small layout systems are lightly bound to the elements around them, each of them often adapts independently of the rest of the design.

If you've read *Responsive Web Design,* this may feel like a bit of a departure. After all, my last book focused on building a page, not the individual components within it (http://bkaprt. com/rdpp/01-15/). Over a few short chapters, it showed how to translate pixel-based designs into fluid, grid-based layouts; how to resize images within those flexible layouts; and finally, how to use media queries to shape those sprawling, fluid designs into finished responsive layouts.

But in many ways, the modules *within* our responsive pages are more challenging than the layouts themselves. Designing a responsive grid is wonderful, but how do we ensure our images are as recognizable on the smallest screens as they are on the widest ones? How can we possibly fit dense, complex navigation menus into fluid layouts? Can we incorporate advertising into our responsive grids without sobbing heavily?

While flexible grids and media queries can answer some of these questions, they're only part of the solution. That's why this book takes a closer look at the challenges of these small

FIG 1.8: The lead stories on Google's Year in Search 2014 have only one breakpoint.

FIG 1.9: Secondary stories change their grid layout across a few breakpoints.

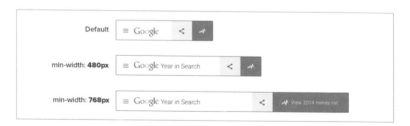

FIG 1.10: The navigation undergoes a few small but noticeable changes, increasing in visual density as it widens.

layout systems, of the modules and elements contained within the page. In each of the chapters that follow , we'll examine an especially challenging component—beginning with navigation, exploring images and video, and finally, advertising. We'll study common (and uncommon) design approaches for each of these modules, and discuss strategies for incorporating those elements into your own responsive designs. As we do, we'll have a better understanding not just of the challenges that await us when designing more modularly, but of the rewards as well.

In many ways, modular design affords us—and our projects—some very tangible benefits. In describing how they rebuilt Capital One's layout in *four weeks,* developer Scott Childs argued that a focus on components, not pages, was key (http:// bkaprt.com/rdpp/01-16/):

Even though it's this massive number of pages, when you look at 2,500 pages over 4,000 page configurations, everything boils down to a couple things really. How many different components do we have total? It's around twenty components.

This component-driven focus on design has grown out of a need for modularity in our work—especially as the scope and complexity of the work increases. Joe Stewart, design partner on Virgin America's responsive redesign, suggested that the benefits weren't just about modularity (http://bkaprt. com/rdpp/01-17/):

We made a system of Legos. We designed different box types, different module types that could work at different sizes. They could work for a tablet or a desktop or a phone and then within there, the content can change. There's a couple of good things about that:

1. *Anything that you do will automatically be responsive. Because if it fits in one of these modules, it will be responsive because the module system itself is naturally responsive.*
2. *The second good thing is Virgin America can now go make whatever pages they want based on these Legos. They can mix and match what's going to work for them so they can*

FIG 1.11: From Ushahidi (http://bkaprt.com/rdpp/01-18/) to MailChimp (http://bkaprt.com/rdpp/01-19/), Starbucks (http://bkaprt.com/rdpp/01-20/) to A List Apart (http://bkaprt.com/rdpp/01-21/), pattern libraries help us manage the components of our responsive interfaces.

---

have two big ones, three small ones, and four or whatever it is. They forever will have this set of tools that is naturally responsive to build out their site.

This talk of building interfaces out of smaller building blocks has, in recent years, been accompanied by a renewed interest in creating *pattern libraries* or *style guides.* I use the terms interchangeably, but whichever one you prefer, the meaning is the same: they're inventories of all the "blocks" used to build more complex interfaces. Those reusable components—whether they be colors, typefaces, form elements, or grid layouts—are frequently referred to as *design patterns,* a nod to their reusable, modular nature. Starbucks was one of the first large organizations to publish a public pattern library for its responsive site, with other companies following suit in the years that followed (**FIG 1.11**).

While this more modular, systems-driven approach to our designs may feel like a shift, especially when compared to our

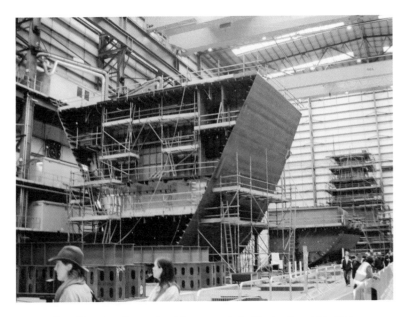

FIG 1.12: A small section of a massive ship, as seen during the boat's construction. Photograph by Adrian Jones (http://bkaprt.com/rdpp/01-22/).

old, page-focused layout models, other industries have been doing it for years. As MailChimp designer Federico Holgado noted (http://bkaprt.com/rdpp/01-23/), fields as diverse as architecture, automotive manufacturing, and shipbuilding long ago shifted their focus to becoming *assemblers of finished components:* of building larger, more complex machines out of smaller, more specialized parts (FIG 1.12). So while it may feel like a change to those of us working on the web, it's also incredibly useful: we can build complex, responsive interfaces in a content-focused, device-agnostic way, readying our designs for an ever-increasing number of browsing contexts.

And frankly, we need to. Because in all honesty, it's been a weird few years for the web.

OKAY, SURE, I could've said that at any point in the web's short history. After all, the only constant about our odd little medium is just how quickly everything changes. But speaking for myself, it feels like the last few years have been especially, well, *nuts* when it comes to device proliferation. A few highlights:

- Mobile is booming, with an estimated 7.4 billion devices on the planet (http://bkaprt.com/rdpp/01-24/). It's quickly become the dominant way for people to access the web—and for large parts of the world, in both developed and developing countries, mobile is the *only* way to access the web. While the popularity of handheld devices shows no signs of slowing down, "mobile" has not, as many predicted, brought about the end of the desktop. Analytics and research firm comScore found that mobile growth "is not coming at the expense of desktop computer usage. [Much of that growth] has been activity...incremental to what's happening on existing platforms" (http://bkaprt.com/rdpp/01-25/).
- It's not just mobile that's defied our expectations. Since the launch of the iPad in 2010, we've seen the tablet market explode, with hardware vendors scrambling to capitalize on the massive popularity of Apple's tablet. At 2011's Consumer Electronics Show alone, there were over eighty new tablet PCs introduced (http://bkaprt.com/rdpp/01-26/).

  More recently, there are signs that the tablet market's starting to soften, with everyone from mobile analysts (http://bkaprt.com/rdpp/01-27/) to Best Buy's CEO (http://bkaprt.com/rdpp/01-28/) suggesting that tablet sales are starting to flatten, if not declining outright.
- 2014 was the year Glass, Google's face-mounted sneezeguard of a wearable computer, tried and failed to gain momentum (http://bkaprt.com/rdpp/01-29/). Even still, there's considerable interest in predicting the next big post-desktop development, from internet-connected smart TVs to, more recently, smart watches.

  Now personally, I'm skeptical of smart watches as a browsing environment. I'm sure that nobody's going to want to interact with long documents on such tiny screens, and that these little devices are probably going to be more

FIG 1.13: Want to browse a responsive site on an Android-based smartwatch? With the Wear Internet Browser, you can (http://bkaprt.com/rdpp/01-30/). Video image from YouTube (http://bkaprt.com/rdpp/01-31/).

useful as notification hubs, connecting other nearby devices more effectively. But whenever I find myself cycling through those objections, I catch myself—because I used to say the same thing about phones. In fact, I was convinced nobody'd ever want to browse the web on a tiny mobile screen. And we already know how that turned out. In fact, many sites are already using wrist-based browsers to great effect (**FIG 1.13**).

In other words, it seems that whenever we start to figure the web out—even a little bit—the landscape shifts.

Although maybe it doesn't so much shift as *explode*. Almost each month, hardware and software vendors introduce new interaction models for us to support in our designs (**FIG 1.14**). New devices and browsing contexts continue to appear faster than we can hope to keep up (**FIG 1.15**). And the network we use to browse the web, publish our work, and connect with our audiences is more widely accessed today than at any other point in the web's short history. But with sub-3G connections comprising the *overwhelming* majority of mobile data subscriptions, that network is also far slower, more volatile, and less reliable

FIG 1.14: Microsoft's Windows 8.1 allows users to split their screen and resize apps to comfortable positions (http://bkaprt.com/rdpp/01-32/).

than we might like to think (**FIG 1.16**). How can responsive design possibly keep up with all of this? More to the point: as responsive designers, how do we?

In this book, we're going to try and answer those questions. While each of the next few chapters focuses on a specific challenge to responsive designers—navigation, images and video, and advertising—we won't just be dissecting layout techniques and code snippets. (Though there will be *plenty* of that, I promise.) As we look at patterns, we'll discuss why they work, their strengths, their weaknesses, and how you might refine them. In the final chapter, we'll review what we've learned and see how we might stitch it together to build more flexible, lightweight layouts—and maybe become more flexible designers, too. If we do our job right, we'll step out of the trees with a clearer view of where we've been and where we're going next.

Let's get started.

FIG 1.15: In a 2009 Ofcom study, 20% of 16- to 24-year-olds in the UK said they used video game consoles to visit websites (http://bkaprt.com/rdpp/01-33/). Photograph by Anna Debenham (http://bkaprt.com/rdpp/01-34/).

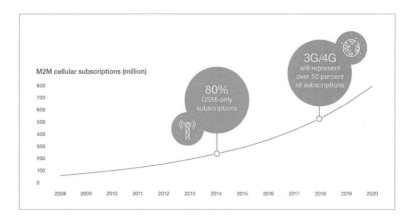

FIG 1.16: Not as fast as we think: Ericsson estimates that more than 80% of the world's data connections are slower than 3G (http://bkaprt.com/rdpp/01-35/, PDF). Image from the November 2014 Ericsson Mobility Report (http://bkaprt.com/rdpp/01-36/).

2 NAVIGATION

" *I may not have gone where I intended to go, but I think I have ended up where I needed to be.*"
—**DOUGLAS ADAMS**, The Long Dark Tea-Time of the Soul

I'VE BEEN READING about a man named Pius "Mau" Piailug who, in 1976, navigated a large voyaging canoe across the Pacific, traveling more than 3,000 miles from Hawai'i to Tahiti. Piailug sailed without the aid of maps, computer-assisted navigation, or any other equipment—instead, he used the stars, sun, and moon to guide him. In fact, the instrument most helpful to him never made it onto his vessel: a star compass, a ring of shells, coral, or pebbles placed around a center point (**FIG 2.1**). The simple-looking instrument helped young navigators of Piailug's tradition understand the relationship between the horizon—the outer ring of the compass—and the canoe in the center. This, coupled with years of training at sea, was what helped Piailug complete his journey, and prove that traditional navigation was still relevant in a modern world.

I think of Piailug's journey often, and of his star compass in particular. Because if we've done our job right, a website's

FIG 2.1: Mau Piailug using a star compass to teach navigation, as he was taught in his youth. Photograph by Monte Costa (http://bkaprt.com/rdpp/02-01/).

navigation should act as a kind of compass: it helps new users orient themselves within a site hierarchy, and guides them to their destination. But with all the different tiers and types of menus our sites contain, designing intuitive, usable navigation can feel like a formidable task.

And those challenges compound themselves when you're designing responsively. How can a complex menu adapt to a smaller screen? What if we want to display more (or less) information depending on the dimensions of the display? Most critically, though, a responsive navigation system doesn't need to look or work the same at every breakpoint, but it does need to offer access to the same content across devices.

These questions might feel daunting, but they demonstrate why navigation is a great example of the *small layout systems* we're going to focus on in this book. The responsive design of a site's navigation poses an almost entirely different challenge than a page's top-level grid. In dealing with challenges of layout, interaction, and visual density, we're forced to ask ourselves: how can we design navigation that's as usable as it is responsive?

FIG 2.2: The responsive navigation for Happy Cog's site seen at sizes wide and small (http://bkaprt.com/rdpp/02-02/).

Thankfully, there are many great attempts at answering that question. In this chapter, we'll look at design patterns both common and not-so-common, and see if we can't find our way through the challenges of responsively designing navigation.

THE SHOW/HIDE TOGGLE

Open up design agency Happy Cog's responsive site (**FIG 2.2**). On wider screens, the entire navigation is visible, but on smaller viewports, where screen real estate is at a premium, the top of the design only shows a Menu link. If you tap, click on, or select that link with your keyboard, the full menu appears.

This is one of the most common ways of handling complex navigation systems in a responsive design: when the menu doesn't fit, conceal it. This pattern requires two elements at minimum: the navigation, which is concealed at certain breakpoints; and a "trigger" element, which the user interacts with to reveal the navigation. In fact, we took the same approach with the menu on responsivewebdesign.com (**FIG 2.3**). The design's fairly modest, but I'll briefly walk you through the code to demonstrate how this pattern's often implemented..

First, at the top of the page, we have this markup:

```
<div class="head">
  <h1 class="logo">
  <a href="/"><img src="/images/logo-rwd.png"
    alt="Responsive Web Design" /></a>
  </h1>

  <div id="nav" class="nav">
    <nav>
    <h1><a class="skip" href="#menu">Explore this
      site:</a></h1>

      <ul id="menu">
        <li><a href="/workshop/">Workshop</a></li>
        <li><a href="/events/">Public Events</a>
        </li>
        <li><a href="/podcast/">Podcast</a></li>
        <li><a href="/newsletter/">Newsletter</a>
        </li>
        <li><a href="/about/">About</a></li>
      </ul>
    </nav>
  </div><!-- /end .nav -->
</div>

<!-- [ The page's main content goes here. ] -->
```

I've simplified things a little, but there's not much more to it: the document leads off with our logo, a link to skip to the navigation, and then the navigation itself, marked up as an unordered list. But that HTML is, as you might have guessed, just the foundation. To enhance the menu further, let's begin with a simple JavaScript test:

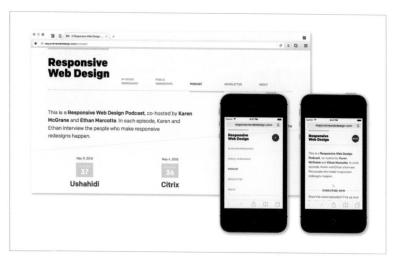

FIG 2.3: The responsive masthead for, uh, responsivewebdesign.com. Straightforward design, with a simple toggle to show (or hide) the navigation.

```
// Is this browser sufficiently modern to continue?
if ( !( "querySelector" in document
   && "addEventListener" in window
   && "getComputedStyle" in window) ) {
    return;
}

window.document.documentElement.className +=
  " enhanced";
```

We're asking the user's browser if it supports the DOM features we'll need elsewhere in our JavaScript—features like document. querySelector, window.addEventListener, and window.get-ComputedStyle. If they're not found, then that return; keeps the browser from executing the rest of our JavaScript. The result is that older browsers are left with a perfectly usable experience, albeit a less JavaScript-enabled one (**FIG 2.4**). And when those features are found, our JavaScript applies a class of enhanced

FIG 2.4: No JavaScript? No problem: our navigation's still accessible, even to modern browsers that can't load our code.

to the HTML element (`window.document.documentElement.className += " enhanced";`).

Why run that test? Well, this JavaScript test lets us build our navigation with a pinch of progressive enhancement: we can design a simpler but *usable* experience that's universally accessible by default, and then enhance the experience *only* for browsers and devices that will actually benefit from it. If the test successfully runs, then the enhanced class on the HTML element tells us a given browser is receiving the "enhanced" experience.

This is a fairly common approach for responsive sites, especially at a certain scale. For example, the BBC News team built their responsive design upon a foundation of progressive enhancement (**FIG 2.5**), using a little JavaScript test similar to the one we've used above, which allows them to determine whether a browser "cuts the mustard" (http://bkaprt.com/rdpp/02-03/):

We make [the browser landscape] manageable in the same [way] you and everyone else in the industry does it: by having a lowest common denominator and developing towards that. So we've taken the decision to split the entire browser market into two, which we are currently calling "feature browsers" and "smart browsers". ...as the [site] loads we earmark incapable

FIG 2.5: The BBC News site is accessible—and responsive—on every internet-connected device, but the experience is slightly enhanced on more modern browsers. Photograph courtesy Responsive News (http://bkaprt.com/rdpp/02-04/).

browsers with the above code and exclude the bulk of the JavaScript-powered UI from them, leaving them with a clean, concise core *experience.*

Instead of tracking myriad combinations of browsers and devices, the BBC can think of their design as existing in one of two broad *experience* tiers: a baseline responsive experience, and a slightly more advanced experience that's only served to the browsers that can handle it.

On a much smaller scale, that's exactly what we're doing with the navigation on responsivewebdesign.com. With that enhanced class in place, we can write more advanced styles directed at the browsers that pass our test, and build the more advanced view of our navigation:

```
.enhanced .nav .skip {
    position: absolute;
    right: 0;
    top: 1.4em;
    background: #363636;
    border-radius: 50%;
    width: 2.5em;
    height: 2.5em;
}
.enhanced .nav ul {
    max-height: 0;
    overflow: hidden;
}
```

If a browser passes our JavaScript test, this rule will use plain ol' absolute positioning to take that skip link before our navigation—.nav .skip—and stick it at the top of the page. At the same time, by applying a pinch of background: #363636 and border-radius: 50%, we can turn that link into a big, gray, circular button. But the second rule is where things get interesting: it selects the ul inside .nav—that is, the unordered list that contains our navigation links—and uses overflow: hidden and max-height: 0 to turn the list into a 0px-tall box, effectively hiding our links from view. Hiding them, that is, until a class of .open is applied to the list:

```
.enhanced .nav ul.open {
    max-height: 20em;
}
```

With those rules, we now have two states for our navigation: completely hidden and expanded (**FIG 2.6**). Sounds great and all, but you might be wondering how we'll get that class on our ul. Well, that's where a little more JavaScript comes into play:

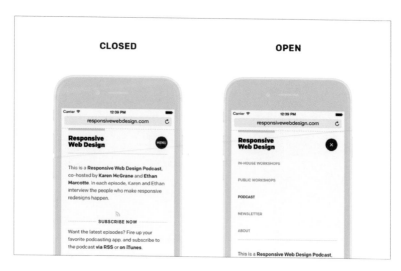

FIG 2.6: Our CSS now allows us to show or hide the navigation. But how do we make it interactive?

```
var nav = document.querySelector( ".nav ul" ),
    navToggle = document.querySelector( ".nav .skip" );

if ( navToggle ) {
  navToggle.addEventListener( "click",
    function( e ) {
    if ( nav.className == "open" ) {
      nav.className = "";
    } else {
    nav.className = "open";
    }

    e.preventDefault();
  }, false );
}
```

If JavaScript's not your thing, don't worry—the code's more straightforward than it looks, I promise. Remember that skip

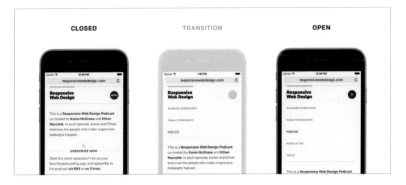

| CLOSED | TRANSITION | OPEN |

FIG 2.7: Why not include a little max-height transition, you say? Great idea!

link inside our .nav element? Well, we're using some JavaScript to look for it (document.querySelector(".nav .skip")) and, if it's found, add some functionality whenever it's clicked or tapped (navToggle.addEventListener("click", …);). When a user taps or clicks on that link, our code checks to see if our unordered list has a class of open (if (nav.className === "open") { … }). If it doesn't, the JavaScript adds the class to reveal the links; and if it *does*, it removes the class, and hides the navigation from view.

And if we want to get a little fancy—and of *course* we want to get a little fancy—we can add a CSS transition on the max-height, allowing the list to subtly telescope in and out of view (**FIG 2.7**):

```
.enhanced .nav ul {
  max-height: 0;
  overflow: hidden;
  transition: max-height 0.25s ease-out;
}
```

And we're done! With a little bit of JavaScript, we can show (or hide) an element of our design when it's clicked on, all by adding (or removing) a class.

(Quick aside: while overflow is a CSS property older than time, it's worth noting that an astonishingly high number of mobile browsers don't implement it correctly. If any part of your design uses overflow: auto to create scrollable areas, I recommend Filament Group's Overthrow.js library (http://bkaprt.com/rdpp/02-05/), which properly detects support for overflow while weeding out the browsers that claim to support the property but don't.)

While the show/hide toggle works beautifully, that doesn't mean the effect's necessarily appropriate for *all* breakpoints. The toggle's really only valuable on smaller viewports, where the layout's a bit tighter; when the viewport gets wider, we can display the entire navigation, locked-up with the logo (**FIG 2.8**). But since the entire effect is driven by our CSS, we can override it above a certain breakpoint with a media query:

```
@media screen and (min-width: 39em) {
  .page .nav ul {
    overflow: auto;
    max-height: inherit;
  }
}
```

Now, when the viewport reaches a minimum width of 39em, we've disabled the overflow: hidden on the list, and returning its max-height to a normal, default value. As a result, our list is no longer hidden from view, allowing us to style it like a more traditional masthead.

...phew!

That might seem like a lot of work, but we're simply adding or removing a class with a little JavaScript, and using that class to control the visibility of our navigation. And really, that's the basic mechanism of nearly all show/hide toggles. MSNBC.com's responsive site does this very thing, in fact (**FIG 2.9**): on widescreen displays, tapping or clicking on the primary categories reveals secondary menus; but on smaller displays, tapping on an icon reveals the entire navigation, with submenus also expandable within it.

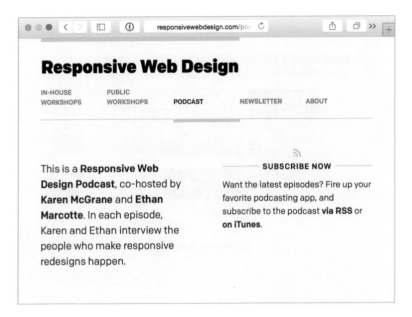

FIG 2.8: For wider screens, we can disable the show/hide toggle, and just keep our links in view.

FIG 2.9: MSNBC's responsive navigation uses a top-level toggle to reveal its menu on smaller screens. Additionally, users can open nested menus by tapping or clicking on the relevant sections.

FIG 2.10: Walmart.ca's navigation is hidden "off-canvas" on narrower viewports, but visible by default on wider ones.

THE OFF-CANVAS MENU

A variant of the show/hide toggle is what's colloquially referred to as the *off-canvas menu*. While this pattern first gained traction in native mobile applications, it's recently seen use in responsive and mobile websites (http://bkaprt.com/rdpp/02-06/). As it happens, Walmart.ca adopted this approach in their recent responsive redesign (**FIG 2.10**). On wider screens, the navigation's visible at the left. But on smaller screens, tapping or clicking on the Shop icon causes the entire navigation to *slide* in from the left, positioned just beyond the visible canvas.

From a mechanical standpoint, this isn't considerably different from our old, trusty show/hide toggle: we're still concealing our navigation, and then asking our users to interact with an element to toggle its visibility. If executed well, the off-canvas menu can convey an extra layer of depth and dimensionality in your layout. It does, however, require extra care to make sure it's built accessibly, and that it doesn't break the experience for all but the latest browsers (http://bkaprt.com/rdpp/02-07/).

CONDITIONALLY LOADED MENUS

FiveThirtyEight.com, an American news and entertainment site, launched a responsive redesign in 2014 (**FIG 2.11**). On smaller displays, their team opted for a show/hide toggle for their navigation. While they kept that toggle on wider viewports, links to their main article categories—Politics, Economics, Science, and so on—are pulled out of the hidden menu, and made visible by default. But there's something else at play here: on wider screens, tapping or clicking links in the masthead reveals a dropdown menu, teasing additional content from that section of the site (**FIG 2.12**).

Here's a high-level look at one item in FiveThirtyEight's navigation menu:

```
<ul class="menu">
  <li class="menu-item">
    <a href="http://fivethirtyeight.com">Menu</a>
    <div class="dropdown">
    <!-- Subnav content goes here -->

    </div>
  </li>
  <!-- Subnav content goes here -->

</ul>
```

Each top-level link sits inside a list item (li.menu-item), which also contains a div with a class of dropdown. And those divs contain—you guessed it!—the dropdown menu that appears on wider screens. That's some straightforward markup, to be sure—but it provides a foundation for the CSS that displays the dropdowns on wider screens:

FIG 2.11: The responsive redesign for FiveThirtyEight.com. As news sites go, it's a stately, analysis-rich affair.

FIG 2.12: FiveThirtyEight's responsive navigation is a simple show/hide toggle on all displays, with key links promoted to the masthead on wider screens.

```
li.menu-item {
  position: relative;
}
.dropdown {
  display: none;
  position: absolute;
}
@media screen and (min-width: 768px) {
  li.menu-item:hover .dropdown {
    display: block;
  }
}
```

I'm simplifying FiveThirtyEight's styles a bit, but the underlying mechanics are still the same: on small screens, the .dropdown blocks are hidden by default with display: none; but by using a media query, they can reveal the menus on wider viewports when someone hovers over the containing list item (li.menu-item:hover .dropdown).

The approach FiveThirtyEight's using here is common, but not without its drawbacks. Relying on :hover is a potential liability, as the CSS assumes all widescreen devices are mouse-enabled. And there are plenty of devices that buck that trend, from tablets to touch-enabled laptops. But more broadly, there's a considerable drawback to using CSS to hide information on smaller screens: namely, that the browser will still download all the HTML for a hidden element, even if the styles hide it from view. In other words, the small screen users of FiveThirtyEight.com—and of other sites that use this display: none pattern—will be downloading extra data they won't use. And if your readers are on a metered data connection, that can be a potentially costly design decision.

A more responsible alternative would be to use conditional loading: to load that extra content only under certain conditions, ensuring it's only loaded on the screens that will use it. When the *Boston Globe*'s responsive site launched, the design team and I adopted a similar pattern for their masthead: on smaller screens, the entire site's navigation would be accessible by toggling its visibility (**FIG 2.13**). But as the design widened

FIG 2.13: When the site first launched, the Boston Globe's responsive navigation toggled its visibility on smaller displays. But on wider displays, the navigation was visible—and included teasers for key stories from each section.

and there was more space to work with, we took advantage of the space to promote key stories in each section.

Most important, those panels aren't available on smaller screens—but their markup isn't included in the page by default, and then hidden with CSS. Instead, the extra HTML is conditionally loaded using a bit of JavaScript. Personally, I quite like Filament Group's Ajax-Include pattern (http://bkaprt.com/rdpp/02-08/) for managing conditionally loaded content:

```
<ul>
  <li data-append="/politics/latest-stories.html"
    data-media="(min-width: 39em)">
    <a href="/politics/">Politics</a>
  </li>
</ul>
```

The Ajax-Include pattern works by applying an HTML5 data- attribute to a part of your HTML, which describes where the conditionally loaded content should be placed (data-before, data-after, data-append, or data-replace); if you like, you can also specify a media query (via the optional data-media attribute) to note that the content should only

FIG 2.14: Certain modules on the Guardian's site used conditional loading to reduce information density across breakpoints.

be loaded *if* certain conditions are met in the client. So in the above snippet, the Ajax-Include JavaScript fetches the content of `/politics/latest-stories.html`, presumably just a snippet of HTML, and *appends* it to our list item—but only if the viewport has a minimum width of `39em`.

As you may have guessed, conditional loading isn't just handy for navigation—it can benefit other types of content as well. The *Guardian,* for example, had several kinds of conditionally loaded content on an earlier version of their site. When viewed on a wider screen, certain lead stories were accompanied by a row of related articles. But when you looked at the same module on a smaller screen, only the lead stories were visible. Now, those secondary stories weren't hidden with a bit of CSS. Instead of taking the performance hit of downloading the content on every device, the site loaded the related articles only if the user's browser supported JavaScript *and* was wider than a specified width (**FIG 2.14**). Otherwise, the most important content—the lead stories—was seen by everyone.

It's worth noting that conditional loading isn't about providing "desktop" users with more content, or "mobile" users with less. Rather, conditional loading can help us address problems of *density* in your design, ensuring that the information shown to our readers never overwhelms them. The Guardian and the Boston Globe have identified the content that's important to *all* of their users, and used that as the basis for both the wide- and small-screen views of each module.

In other words, it's not about removing or hiding extra information on smaller screens. Instead, try thinking about your content through this three-part framework:

1. Identify the content critical to the smaller screen.
2. Once you've done that, consider that content to be the information accessible to all your readers, regardless of how wide (or small) their screen happens to be.
3. If there's additional information you'd like to include on wider viewports, consider it an *enhancement*.

Adopting this "mobile first" mindset won't necessarily change the implementation, but it will inform the way you plan the design of your conditionally loaded content. It'll help avoid the trap of thinking of smaller screens as somehow deserving of "less" content—especially when our audiences are becoming increasingly (if not exclusively) mobile-oriented.

HOUSTON, WE MAY HAVE A HAMBURGER PROBLEM

As you've seen in this chapter so far, there's no truly perfect way to manage navigation. And this isn't an exhaustive list of navigation patterns: everyone from Filament Group (http://bkaprt.com/rdpp/02-09/) to Mozilla (http://bkaprt.com/rdpp/02-10/) has weighed in on various approaches to building responsive, multi-device-friendly navigation systems.

But as distinct as these approaches are, many of them happen to share one element in common (**FIG 2.15**). Namely, an icon of three stacked, horizontal bars, colloquially—and perhaps unfortunately—referred to as the "hamburger": ☰.

According to Quora (http://bkaprt.com/rdpp/02-11/) and the BBC (http://bkaprt.com/rdpp/02-12/), our little hamburger icon

FIG 2.15: Behold the "hamburger": a common icon toggle for responsive navigation systems.

was first used digitally on the Xerox Star, a little workstation that launched in 1981 and established a number of standards for modern personal computing: a multi-button mouse, windows-based graphical interfaces, and the like (**FIG 2.16**).

At the time, the ≡ icon was used to open a contextually relevant menu. But more recently, it's been used as a trigger to reveal a site's entire navigation, especially at smaller resolutions. And there are some real benefits to working with the icon: it's incredibly compact, and is quite legible even on smaller screens; also, it's very easy to include it in your designs, whether using SVG (http://bkaprt.com/rdpp/02-13/), some fancy CSS-based animations (http://bkaprt.com/rdpp/02-14/), or a plain ol' HTML entity (☰).

But as wonderful as the hamburger is, and as ubiquitous as it seems to be, I'm here to suggest that it might have some problems. And maybe we should talk about them a bit—preferably before we slap the icon on all of our responsive sites.

(Also, is anyone else hungry?)

LET'S BEGIN WITH the responsive website for *Time* magazine (http://bkaprt.com/rdpp/02-15/). Launched in 2014, it features a layout as flexible as its aesthetic is bold. (**FIG 2.17**). And while

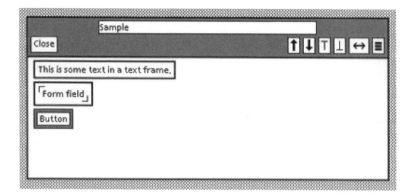

FIG 2.16: The hamburger's gotten a lot more mileage lately, but was first seen on screens in the early 1980s, as part of the Xerox Star's graphical interface (http://bkaprt.com/rdpp/02-11/).

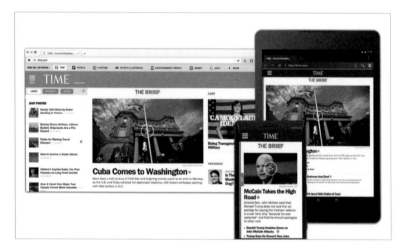

FIG 2.17: The newly responsive website for *Time,* as flexible as it is fashionable (http://bkaprt.com/rdpp/02-15/).

Time's pages are packed with content, they never overwhelm: the design's simple palette and clear hierarchy allows the reader to quickly identify the stories most relevant to her, regardless of how small—or large—her screen might be.

One aspect of the redesign I find especially impressive is the sheer amount of navigation on each page. (I should note I've never been accused of being especially "cool.") There are, as best as I can tell, four separate navigation elements on the homepage:

1. On wider viewports, a menubar appears at the top of the page, allowing the user to leap to other sites in the Time Inc. network (**FIG 2.18**).
2. The page's footer contains a list of links to core sections of the website (**FIG 2.19**).
3. Supplemental content appears on the left edge of the page. On the homepage, for example, you see a feed of recent stories, a stock ticker, and *Time*'s site search. But that's just the *widescreen* view of this part of the design. On smaller screens, there's a tab labeled "TAP" that allows the user to open the content as a panel, which covers the page. When they're finished, they can tap or click on the tab to close it (**FIG 2.20**).
4. The primary navigation is concealed until a user taps or clicks on the hamburger icon. On smaller viewports, the navigation covers the entire design. On wider screens, the drawer covers the left side of the page (**FIG 2.21**).

Sounds like quite a lot, doesn't it? But again, I think *Time* balances the density well. Noisier navigation menus are concealed when space is at a premium, and as the screen gets progressively wider, each menu is shown by default *only when there's sufficient space to do so*. But the one navigation element that's *always* hidden on all breakpoints is, interestingly, the site's primary navigation. Yes, that's right: it's tucked behind our beloved hamburger icon.

In fact, when the responsive TIME.com first launched, the hamburger was treated in a fairly novel way: when the page loaded for the first time, an overlay appeared next to the icon, informing the reader that she could use the icon to reveal the site's navigation. What's more, if her browser had a mouse, she

FIG 2.18: The menu at the top of the page is conditionally loaded on wider viewports, treating it as a widescreen enhancement.

FIG 2.19: Behold *Time*'s footer. Dense, perhaps, but rich with relevant links.

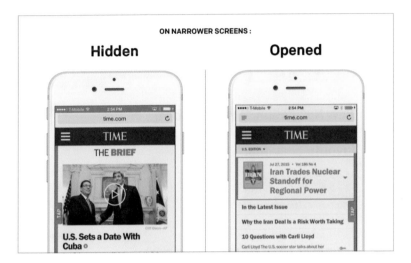

FIG 2.20: Less critical content is placed in a drawer that's shown by default on wider screens. But on smaller screens, it's concealed by default until a user taps or clicks to reveal it.

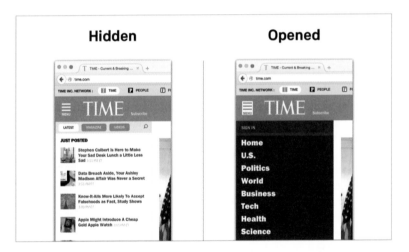

FIG 2.21: *Time*'s primary navigation is the real showpiece, hidden behind a hamburger icon.

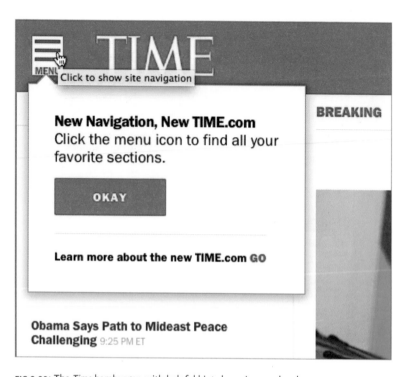

FIG 2.22: The *Time* hamburger, with helpful hints hovering overhead.

could also hover over the icon for a helpful tooltip informing her she could "Click to show site navigation." (FIG 2.22). In other words, the icon had *three* separate levels of text explaining it: the "Menu" label, the overlay, and the tooltip. While I don't have any insights into the redesign, this degree of explanation suggests a couple of possible motives: either the site's stakeholders weren't confident in the icon's ability to clearly identify itself as a critical navigation element, or the hamburger icon didn't perform well in usability tests before launch.

Once again, I'm conjecturing. But if *Time* did uncover usability issues with their use of the hamburger icon, they wouldn't be the first to do so. Designer James Foster ran a thorough usability study on a large site's responsive navigation, and found that the word "Menu" consistently outperformed the icon alone, with a 12.9% higher conversion rate (http://bkaprt.com/rdpp/02-16/). As a result, his team abandoned the hamburger icon, and moved to a slightly more verbose trigger for their responsive navigation. It's not just happening on websites, either. The designers of Beamly's native app discovered that ditching hideable drawers in favor of always-visible navigation dramatically improved user engagement and satisfaction (http://bkaprt.com/rdpp/02-17/).

This isn't to say that our ubiquitous little icon can't be successful. (Heck, it's presumably performing quite well for *Time*.) In fact, the UX team at Booking.com recently surveyed their users and found the hamburger icon worked just fine for their site *and* its audience (http://bkaprt.com/rdpp/02-18/). In fact, changing the icon to the word "Menu" had no significant impact on their users' behavior.

So some sites say the hamburger's no good for them, while others say it's perfectly fine—what gives? In the face of some seemingly incompatible results, I think this demonstrates that the hamburger icon, like all design patterns, is worth testing on *your* site. When he shared his defense of the hamburger icon, Booking.com's Michel Ferreira said it best:

There is a lesson here for all of us on the nature of A/B testing. You are never solely testing a UI element, pattern, or feature. You are testing these things against a very specific user base in a very specific scenario. What works for Booking.com may not work for you and your users. This is the reason we A/B test in the first place, because the findings of others…are all unproven until they've been tested against our customers, on our platform.

Beautifully said. There's nothing inherently wrong with the hamburger icon itself—but assuming it's a safe default for *every* responsive navigation system can be problematic. After all, what works for one site may not work for yours. So by all means, hamburger your sites! Just be sure to test those hamburgers before serving them up to your audience.

THE DRAWER DILEMMA

But let's put our icon issues aside for a moment. Because there's another, possibly larger problem with our ability to conceal navigation.

Regard the responsive Disney.com, launched in 2012. And as responsive looks go, it's, well, lovely: replete with lavish images, videos, and content from Disney's various companies, it's an immersive, well-presented piece of responsive design, especially for such a well-known brand (**FIG 2.23**). And as with most responsive sites these days, they decided to hamburger their navigation. On smaller and midsize breakpoints, tapping on the hamburger reveals their site navigation which, if you'll count, contains every link ever created on the World Wide Web (**FIG 2.24**). I saw a Geocities page I designed in 1998 somewhere in there, three or four levels deep.

...okay, I'm trolling. (Sorry, Mickey.) But I hope it's clear I'm trolling out of *love*. Because while the layout and aesthetics of Disney's navigation are skillfully executed, their design illustrates a larger problem with concealing navigation: that, given the option to hide them, our menus can easily become filled with an overwhelming (and perhaps unhelpful) number of links. In discussing common design issues in apps for iOS, Mike Stern, a user experience evangelist at Apple, covered a number of the issues with hidden navigation drawers (http://bkaprt.com/rdpp/02-19/). While most of his design critiques are most pertinent to iOS apps, his last point is relevant to any digital designer, whether native- or web-focused:

> *And finally, the downside of being able to show a lot of options is that you can show a lot of options. Is that you will show a lot of options. The potential for bloat and misuse is tremendous... Look, drawers of any kind have a nasty tendency to fill with junk.*

I couldn't agree more. Like many responsive sites that collapse their navigation, Disney's navigation drawer is visually lovely, but suffers from an overabundance of content. That's why conditionally revealed navigation patterns work best when

FIG 2.23: Disney.com: responsively redesigned, and gorgeously so.

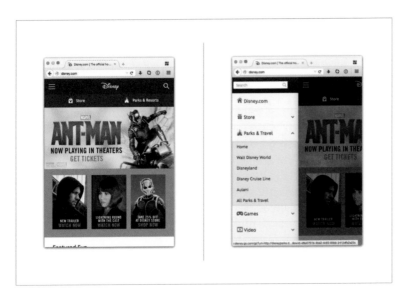

FIG 2.24: Disney's gradual reveal of their navigation, seen here *avec* hamburger.

paired with an almost aggressive curation of the content inside them. In fact, in his original essay on "mobile first," Luke Wroblewski notes that beginning a design project with smaller screens is a boon to products—and to their users (http://bkaprt.com/rdpp/02-20/) (emphasis mine):

> Mobile devices require software development teams to focus on only the most important data and actions in an application. There simply isn't room in a 320 by 480 pixel screen for extraneous, unnecessary elements. You have to prioritize. So when a team designs mobile first, the end result is an experience focused on the key tasks users want to accomplish without the extraneous detours and general interface debris that litter today's desktop-accessed Web sites. That's good user experience and good for business.

"You have to prioritize." That's the key point—we should use small screens as a lens through which we view every aspect of our designs, including our navigation. And if we're collapsing or hiding something because it doesn't "fit," let's instead see that as an opportunity to stop and ask if there's a larger issue at play: that is, if we're hiding or removing an element because it doesn't have value on smaller screens, can we simplify the design and content of that element until it works on smaller screens? Or, alternately, maybe it doesn't have value for *any* screen?

And really, I think that's the primary reason it feels so difficult to work with responsive navigation systems: they're often designed from a desktop-first mindset, and we're left to make them "fit" on smaller screens. But if our users are opening our navigation drawers and finding all the junk we didn't want to sift through in our redesign, is that show/hide toggle really benefiting anyone?

To be clear: I think the ability to conditionally conceal parts of a design is incredibly useful, especially for navigation. Whisking away unnecessary information and features can reduce the cognitive load on our users, and make our sites more approachable. But that useful ability is also easily *mis*used. If we're truly designing mobile-first, we shouldn't use show/hide toggles to sidestep the potentially difficult discussions about the real value of our content.

After all, if our audiences are becoming predominantly mobile, we should stop trying to make complex, widescreen-designed elements play nice on smaller screens—instead, we should consider the small-screen user's needs first.

ALTERNATIVE PATTERNS

Of course, there's real value in using widely-adopted design patterns. If a symbol like the hamburger icon is familiar to your users because they've used it elsewhere, it can lower the barrier of entry, and make your navigation more intuitive to them. And that's not something we should devalue lightly: the familiarity of an element can be a powerful benefit, both to our sites and to our audiences.

However, we shouldn't evaluate the utility of design patterns on their ubiquity alone. Patterns are, after all, just patterns: they're not rules or defaults. In fact, there are some rather novel alternative navigation patterns out there. Let's take a look at a few of them.

The progressive reveal

The visual state of our responsive navigation is often treated as somewhat binary: it's either entirely visible or completely hidden. But some sites are challenging that approach, and designing navigation systems that make the best possible use of the space available to them.

The BBC has been experimenting with responsive design in public for some time now, redesigning the m-dot site for BBC News to be completely responsive. While their responsive design was initially accessible only to their mobile audience, it eventually became the default experience for all their users— whether on mobile, tablet, desktop, or anything else (http:// bkaprt.com/rdpp/02-21/; **FIG 2.25**).

The site has two levels of navigation: global navigation at the top for other sites in the BBC network, and then a menu below

FIG 2.25: Flexible, fast, and resilient: the responsive site for BBC News began as a mobile-only site, and then became the default experience for all of their users.

it for BBC News-specific links (FIG 2.26). I think it's safe to say that neither menu is light on content, but rather than simply concealing their navigation, they've adopted a *progressive reveal* pattern for it. At the smallest level, each menu contains a single element that toggles the display of additional links: the topmost menu has a "More" link, while the BBC News navigation has a hamburger-enabled "Sections" link.

But as both navigation menus gradually widen, things get interesting: instead of simply moving the trigger around, each navigation bar gradually reveals links from its hidden panel. Anything that's still hidden is accessible by tapping or clicking on the "More" link or the "Sections" button—and as the design gets wider still, more links are gradually, *progressively* revealed. So while the global navigation menu might show "News" and "Sport" links at a smaller breakpoint, a slightly wider viewport might then promote "Weather," "Shop," and "Earth" as well (FIG 2.27).

As you may have guessed, this is a JavaScript-driven solution. When the page loads, resizes, or gets reoriented in a handheld browser, the BBC measures the width of the browser's viewport and then, based on its width, shows or hides certain links in each menu. The panels that expand when you tap or click on

FIG 2.26: The two levels of navigation on the BBC News site, viewed at a few different breakpoints.

"More" or "Sections" are JavaScript-generated too, populated with any links that happen to be hidden in the parent menu at that breakpoint.

The *Guardian* uses a similar approach for their navigation. While their menu relies more on CSS than JavaScript, it embraces some of the same principles of progressively revealing links over time. In a post on their developer blog, product manager Chris Mulholland described the menu as a hybrid solution: one that combines the show/hide toggle seen on most

FIG 2.27: As with the global navigation, the BBC News-specific menu progressively reveals links over time—while ensuring the remainder are always accessible from the "More" dropdown.

responsive sites, while still keeping key elements visible at all times (http://bkaprt.com/rdpp/02-22/):

> We have prioritised the signposting at smaller screen widths, but the side-scrolling allows you to access any sibling or top-level section.

If side-scrolling isn't your thing, the All Sections is a familiar 'safety-net', giving you access across the site, starting with the section you are in.

We have also tried to make it easier to navigate through the subsections, for example in Culture you are always shown the next section in the sequence. The links loop around almost like a carousel—making it easier to click through the sections.

Rather than simply concealing the navigation entirely, the *Guardian* opted to present top-level categories in a scrollable container (**FIG 2.28**). As you might imagine, this scrollable area gets quite small on narrow viewports, but still allows the user to move through the carousel-like layout to find information most relevant to her. But if she doesn't find what she's looking for, regardless of viewport sizes, there's an "All Sections" link, which reveals a complex, multilevel navigation structure for the entire site (**FIG 2.29**).

Generally speaking, the navigation's structure doesn't change considerably as the design reshapes itself. You can view the site on the narrowest smartphone or the widest flatscreen display, and you're still left with the same scrollable region, with the expandable menu to the right. Given the other navigation patterns we've looked at in this chapter, the *Guardian*'s is almost novel in its consistency.

Becoming more responsive

Putting the technical details aside, what I especially like about the *Guardian*'s navigation is the process of *how* they developed it. If we return to Chris Mulholland's overview of the navigation, he credits their menu design to three factors: a close analysis of their design goals; rapid iteration of a number of possible solutions; and—perhaps most important—involving their users as early as possible in the design process (http://bkaprt.com/rdpp/02-22/):

We know that as much as we can guess and assume what our readers want, there is nothing better than putting prototypes in front of them as early as possible. From the Guardian *web-*

FIG 2.28: The *Guardian* has adopted a different kind of progressive reveal for their navigation.

FIG 2.29: On viewports small or wide, the *Guardian*'s navigation features a toggle to display a complex map of the site's structure.

site, we invited daily visitors to join a panel of users to help us create the new website and provide feedback on ideas. Sending through low-fi prototypes to that panel of users was really valuable...[Next] we developed a prototype that would work with content and was completely realistic...User testing gave us some surprising results and took us down some other paths, but in the end we had much more confidence that regular and new users could navigate to both the most obvious, and the most hidden sections.

In describing his work on the design of Virgin America's new responsive site, Joe Stewart, partner at the design agency Work & Co, said something similar—namely, that prototyping didn't just shape the design process, it *was* the design process. What's more, the client was never shown a static mockup of a web page (http://bkaprt.com/rdpp/02-23/):

Prototyping is basically our number one tool. So our philosophy on how to go about a project like [Virgin America] is to race to a prototype as quickly as possible. We actually never really made a presentation ever once, but we did constantly work on making prototypes. So, even the very first time we got to meet Dean and the Virgin America team, we showed them a responsive prototype.

In recent years, there's been considerable discussion about whether or not we should start "designing in the browser" by leaping right into HTML and CSS—not just to prototype layouts, but to actually begin our creative work directly in the browser. And there are real benefits to that: the browser is, after all, a completely flexible canvas, and no desktop design application currently exists that can match its inherent responsiveness.

I agree with these statements—up to a point. After all, I think the approach has to be paired with the designer. If you're more comfortable thinking in HTML and CSS, great! But if you happen to work more quickly in a traditional design application, there's no reason to abandon a tried and trusted app for your nearest code editor. Instead, it's more important to acknowledge that each tool has strengths and weaknesses, and whichever path gets you to a responsive design first is the one you should take. Joe Stewart said as much during the Virgin America interview:

I still use Photoshop just because it's what I'm fastest in. I know a lot of people are switching to things like Sketch, which seems great, but for me it's just not the fastest. My design partner, Felipe, uses Illustrator for everything because that's what he's fastest in. I think it doesn't really matter how you get there. If you can get something that you can put in a person's hand

and get feedback, that's the goal. However you get there is how you get there.

As much discussion as there is around "designing in the browser," we're not talking about the end of comps as a design tool. As the Virgin America redesign showed, applications like Photoshop and Sketch are still invaluable for sketching, for thinking about layout, for refining and discussing aesthetics. Instead, I think we're seeing the lessening importance of comps as an *end point:* as a client-facing design document or the definitive deliverable. Digital agencies and design teams still use Photoshop or Illustrator mockups to discuss aesthetics or composition options—but our industry still lacks a design tool that reflects the instability of the networks we design for, the various interaction modes available on our users' devices, and the flexibility of the web's canvas.

Personally, I share my colleague Dan Mall's take—we shouldn't necessarily be concerned with designing in the browser, but *deciding* in the browser (http://bkaprt.com/rdpp/02-24/). If you're comfortable sketching in Illustrator or prototyping interactions in Keynote, you should continue to do so. But as the *Guardian*'s Mulholland said, the more quickly you can get your designs into devices and browsers that you, your clients and stakeholders, and your users can hold and interact with, the better:

> We know that as much as we can guess and assume what our readers want, there is nothing better than putting prototypes in front of them as early as possible.

Truer words were never hamburgered—I mean, *spoken.* Whenever possible, we should prioritize prototypes over Photoshop documents. As valuable as comps can be—and they are valuable—there's no substitute for reviewing prototypes "live" in as many browsers and devices as possible. They'll help you vet your design assumptions, and verify you're on the right path.

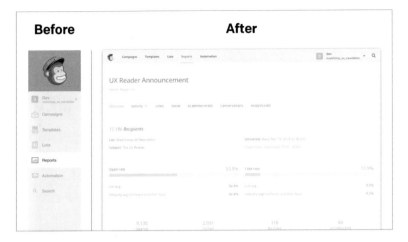

Before **After**

FIG 2.30: The navigation for MailChimp's application, before and after its simplification (http://bkaprt.com/rdpp/02-25/).

Adapt the layout

Even with the best intentions, plans, and processes, our design assumptions don't always play out. When that happens, we often need to revisit parts of our work—and this is especially true of responsive navigation systems. The *Guardian* team landed on their current approach after a considerable amount of iteration. (And I'm sure they'll continue to refine it, too.) Email provider MailChimp found that their web app's responsive navigation, featuring a fixed toolbar, often obscured other interface elements (http://bkaprt.com/rdpp/02-25/). Simplifying the layout didn't just fix those issues—it dramatically improved the menu's usability (**FIG 2.30**).

Perhaps more important, MailChimp's work suggests an alternative to the navigation patterns we've reviewed thus far: rather than taking a complex approach, maybe we should look for opportunities to do less. In fact, we don't always need to

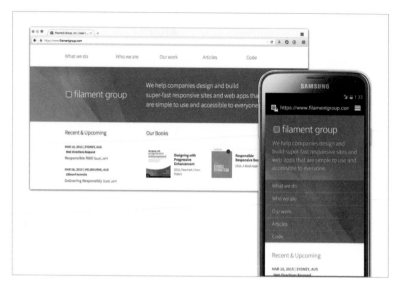

FIG 2.31: Filament Group's navigation isn't just attractive—it's never hidden from view on the homepage (http://bkaprt.com/rdpp/02-26/).

hide or conceal our navigation, when simply changing its layout can be incredibly effective.

Filament Group's responsive site does this admirably. On the homepage, their navigation's never hidden. On wider screens, it's located at the top of the page—but on narrower viewports, the menu's links are stacked directly underneath the company's logo and tagline (**FIG 2.31**). Given how focused their navigation is, this feels like a natural choice: the links can provide valuable signposting, so they're treated as first-class citizens.

As you'll notice, that's *just* on the homepage. On internal pages, Filament adopted a show/hide toggle on smaller screens, allowing them to conserve some much-needed space (**FIG 2.32**). Once again, I think this is a fine choice: since the inner pages' content should be the primary focus, moving the navigation behind a collapsible element makes sense. More important, it neatly demonstrates that patterns don't have to be universally applied throughout a site. Instead, we can be selective and

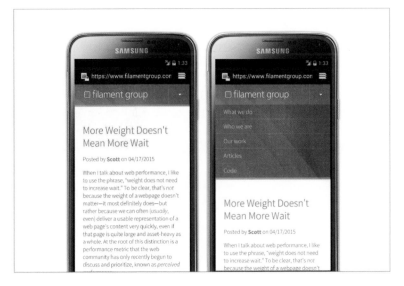

FIG 2.32: On internal pages, Filament Group uses an expandable menu link to conceal their navigation on smaller screens, allowing the content to take center stage.

nuanced in deciding how, where, and why we use those patterns in our work.

Frank Chimero's responsive design is one of my favorites—because, well, *look at it*—but I especially love how he's adopted a similarly reserved approach for his navigation (**FIG 2.33**). No matter how massive or microscopic your screen might be, the navigation's never hidden from view. What's more, Frank spent a considerable amount of time ensuring the navigation doesn't just fit; it feels at home.

Now by most menus' standards, both of these sites' navigations are fairly lightweight—just a handful of links, really. But that's perhaps where they gain a bit of flexibility. A more comprehensive set of links might need a heavier touch, and require adopting a complex design pattern—even (gasp!) a *hamburger!* But instead, I think the lighter touch they've adopted comes not out of their clever design, but out of their focused, distilled content.

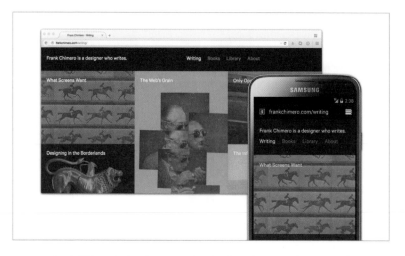

FIG 2.33: Frank Chimero's stunning responsive site, featuring a nav that never quits—or hides (http://bkaprt.com/rdpp/02-27/).

That's not to say responsive navigation systems can't be elegant *and* complex, as the BBC and the *Guardian* have shown. But I suspect that with all the challenges we face on the web, we should constantly search for opportunities to simplify our interfaces. If our responsive navigation can do that, we'll be in a better position to show our users the way.

3 IMAGES AND VIDEOS

So many of the films made today are photographs of people talking."
—**ALFRED HITCHCOCK** (http://bkaprt.com/rdpp/03-01/)

THERE'S BEEN A CONSIDERABLE AMOUNT of writing about how to produce images as flexible as our layouts. In fact, all it takes is a single line of CSS:

```
img {
  max-width: 100%;
}
```

First discovered by designer Richard Rutter, this single rule says that our images can render at whatever dimensions they want, *as long as* their width never exceeds the width of their containing element. In other words, every image's `max-width` is now set to 100% of its container's `width` (http://bkaprt.com/rdpp/03-02/). If that container gets smaller than the width of the image inside it, our industrious little `img` will resize proportionally, never escaping its flexible column.

FIG 3.1: A lead image from an article on the BBC News website. As the article's width changes, the image's max-width: 100% allows it to resize proportionally (http://bkaprt. com/rdpp/03-03/).

Alongside fluid grids and media queries, fluid images are one of the three primary ingredients of a responsive layout. And as a result, they're nearly ubiquitous—open any responsive site, like the BBC News' lovely responsive layout, and you'll find images that expand and contract within their containers (**FIG 3.1**).

For me, it's helpful to think of max-width: 100% as only part of the story: there are issues of performance, delivery, and design, and we'll cover each in this chapter. In other words, creating *fluid* images is just the first step toward creating more *responsive* images. But before we abandon layout entirely, it's worth mentioning that images aren't the only game in town; after all, our designs need to incorporate other kinds of media, like video. So let's take a moment to make our videos as flexible as our images, and continue from there.

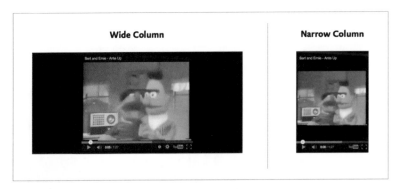

FIG 3.2: Nothing's ever easy on the web: setting our embedded videos to max-width: 100% doesn't *quite* work (http://bkaprt.com/rdpp/03-04/).

TOWARD FLUID VIDEOS

After the past few years of making flexible images, `max-width: 100%` might feel like a natural solution for fluid videos. Unfortunately, it's not quite as easy as that:

```
img,
object,
video {
  max-width: 100%;
}
```

We've extended our CSS slightly, including embedded `objects` and `videos` in our flexible rule. While this works, it doesn't *really* work. If we apply this rule to every video in our responsive layouts, the width of those videos expands and contracts alongside our fluid grid, but the *height* remains fixed (**FIG 3.2**). To see why, let's take a look at the markup behind our movie:

```
<video src="video-main.mp4" height="547"
  width="972"></video>
```

FIG 3.3: Made By Hand, an exquisitely responsive design for an equally moving film series (http://bkaprt.com/rdpp/03-05/).

(A quick note: some third-party services might ask you to use an `object` or `iframe` when embedding their video. The following technique will work for those elements as well, but we'll be sticking with `video` for this demo.)

The markup seems pretty straightforward: the `src` of our `video` element points to, *ahem,* a video file (`video-main.mp4`), while the `width` and `height` attributes determine the dimensions at which our movie should render. But with videos, those last two attributes aren't optional—because unlike images, videos and other embedded objects don't have intrinsic dimensions, so we have to specify them in our HTML. And while we can use `max-width: 100%` to override our video's `width`, we can't do the same with `height`: if we used, say, `height: auto`, our videos would collapse to zero pixels in height and be invisible. And darn it, the internet *needs* its cat videos to be visible.

But luckily, there are a whole host of approaches to making videos resize properly, many of which involve a little light JavaScript. For example, take a look at the responsive site for Made By Hand, a beautiful set of short films featuring rather

FIG 3.4: Relying on JavaScript for proportional videos is fine, but it's not as smooth as a CSS-only approach—our script causes a slight stutter as our design resizes.

inspirational individuals (**FIG 3.3**). (Responsive or not, the film series is visually stunning and emotionally moving. I highly recommend it.) Since the site's responsive, you can view their videos right in your browser, no matter how wide or small your screen might be. To do so, the site's designers wrote a pinch of JavaScript to measure the video when the page first loads, and store the dimensions for future use. After that, whenever the page resizes itself—or the orientation of a device changes—the video resizes proportionally, using calculations based on those initial measurements.

Many responsive sites have adopted similar JavaScript-enabled tactics. Unfortunately, if you resize your browser while using these sites, you might notice a slight visual stutter. As the design resizes, it often takes a fraction of a second for the video to catch up (**FIG 3.4**). This is partially a performance issue: tying JavaScript to the `resize` event can slow down browsers, or potentially even crash them. But it also underscores the problem in relying on JavaScript for critical parts of our layouts. A significant population of mobile users relies on browsers that offer limited or no JavaScript—and on unstable cellular networks, there's no guarantee our JavaScript will even reach our users.

Thankfully, building completely fluid videos is a solved problem. What's more, it doesn't require a lick of JavaScript. You see, way back in 2009, Thierry Koblentz wrote an article demonstrating how to create videos that resize proportionally in flexible layouts (http://bkaprt.com/rdpp/03-06/). And his approach is, frankly, ingenious.

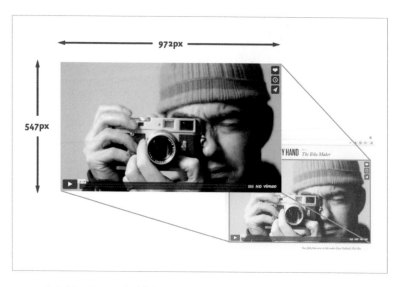

FIG 3.5: Behold a video, embedded in a web page. (I feel like an announcer on one of those wildlife shows.)

Let us pause, if only for a moment, to regard a video on a website. This could be any website, but the homepage for the Made By Hand film series is as good as any (**FIG 3.5**). If we view that page at a viewport width of, say, 1024px, the video's dimensions are 972×547—that is, 972px wide and 547px tall.

But if we look past the pixels, we're really trying to preserve the relationship between two characteristics of our video— namely, its width and its height. And as it happens, those two measurements have a deep and fundamental connection to each other: the *aspect ratio,* measured from one corner of the video to its diagonal opposite (**FIG 3.6**). Luckily for us, we can calculate that aspect ratio by using a simple formula:

```
height ÷ width = aspect ratio
```

If we plug in the dimensions of our 972×547 video, we're left with the following:

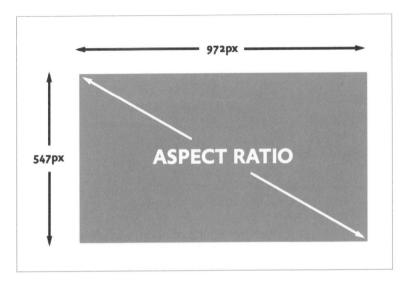

FIG 3.6: The aspect ratio of images and movies describes the relationship between the element's width and its height.

```
547 ÷ 972 = 0.562757202
```

By dividing the height of our video (547px) by its width (972px), we're left with an aspect ratio of 56.2757202%. So as the video resizes, the height of the video should remain roughly 56% of the video's width.

We'll come back to that percentage in a bit, so put it in your back pocket for now. (Or your cargo shorts, if that's your metaphorical legwear of choice. No judgment.) With the math out of the way, let's go back to the video element in our HTML:

```
<video src="video-main.mp4" height="547"
    width="972"></video>
```

As simple as this markup is, let's make two small adjustments to it:

```
<div class="player">
  <video src="video-main.mp4" height="168"
    width="300"></video>
</div>
```

Not much has changed, but we've sized the video down considerably, setting its `width` and `height` to be small-screen-friendly by default. (After all, there's no need to plop a massive video onto smaller screens, right?) More significantly, we've added a little more markup: namely, there's an element wrapped around our `video` element—we've chosen a `div` with a class of `player` here, but the container could be anything you want.

But once it's combined with the aspect ratio we measured previously, that unassuming container is the key to making our video responsive. Let's begin by applying some styles to the outermost `div`:

```
.player {
  padding-top: 56.2757202%;
}
```

Okay, maybe not so much "styles" as "style": with one rule, we've added a `padding-top` equal to the aspect ratio we calculated earlier. But why, you might ask? Well, according to the CSS specification, percentages on `padding-top` and `padding-bottom` are relative to the *width* of the containing block, not the height (http://bkaprt.com/rdpp/03-07/). As a result, that vertical padding will always be `56.2757202%` of the box's width.

Here's a quick example: I've rooted around in my browser's inspector, and removed the video from the Made By Hand homepage. I also disabled the JavaScript that resized the video, *and* added that `padding-top` to its container. And finally, because I am a very professional web designer, I added a not-at-all-garish background color (**FIG 3.7**). But as we resize the design, the `padding-top` resizes as well: it's always roughly 56% of the container's width. In other words, our container `div` might be completely empty, but it has an intrinsic aspect ratio. No matter how wide or small that block gets, its height

FIG 3.7: By applying the aspect ratio as a percentage-based `padding-top` to our container, we've created an empty "ghost box."

FIG 3.8: As we resize our `padding-top`-enabled box, it maintains the shape and proportion our video needs, without a single scrap of content inside.

will always be `56.2757202%` as tall as its width. The empty area created by our `padding-top` is *aspect ratio-aware* (**FIG 3.8**).

Pretty darned cool, right? Well, I think it's cool. (I might have just figured out why I'm never invited to any parties.) But it's only the foundation for our flexible video. With that percentage-based `padding-top` in place, we can go back to our CSS and add a few more styles:

FIG 3.9: With some proportional math and a little extra markup, our video is now resizing responsively—all without a single line of JavaScript.

```
.player {
  position: relative;
  padding-top: 56.2757202%;
}
.player video {
  position: absolute;
  left: 0;
  top: 0;
  height: 100%;
  width: 100%;
}
```

To begin, we've added `position: relative` to the `.player` container. This creates what's known as a *positioning context:* any element absolutely positioned inside the context of that container will now be positioned relative to `.player`, rather than the viewport. And that's what allows the second rule to work: we're positioning the `video` in the top left corner of `.player`. Immediately after that, we're setting the video's `width` and `height` to `100%`, which ensures that they'll be equal to the width and height of their containing element.

If we return to our browser and reinstate the video, we can see the final effect in action (**FIG 3.9**). Remember, that container has an intrinsic aspect ratio: thanks to the percentage-based `padding-top`, the height of our `.player` box will resize proportionally, no matter how wide it becomes. With that in place, we've taken our video and—with some absolute positioning—stretched it across the entirety of our container. And the effect is much, much smoother than if we'd relied on JavaScript.

With nothing more than a little proportional math and an extra container, we've got fluid videos resizing seamlessly within a responsive design.

WORKING WITH FLEXIBLE BACKGROUNDS

`max-width: 100%` is, of course, wonderful—but only for inline images. For flexible background images, we have a number of helpful CSS properties available to us—most notably, `background-size`.

Typically, when we're applying background images to an element, we're asking the browser to render that image at its native resolution. Here's a fairly basic `background` rule:

```
.intro {
  background: url("bg-demo.jpg") no-repeat;
}
```

The browser will apply `bg-demo.jpg` to our `.intro` block, and render that image at its native dimensions. And that's the outcome regardless of whether the image in our rule is four thousand pixels wide or fourteen—if the image happens to be wider or taller than the containing block, the extra pixels won't be displayed.

However, we can override that behavior with the `background-size` property, which allows us to specify the size we'd like our images to display at. We can specify lengths as well, ensuring that our image displays at `250×400`:

```
.intro {
  background: url("bg-demo.jpg") no-repeat;
  background-size: 250px 400px;
}
```

Alternately, if we specify one of the lengths as `auto`, the image will scale proportionally to a specific width or height. For example, a `background-size` of `250px auto` sets our image's width to `250px` without distorting its aspect ratio:

```
.intro {
  background: url("bg-demo.jpg") no-repeat;
  background-size: 250px auto;
}
```

We can even define our `background-size` in percentages, scaling the image relative to the dimensions of its container. So if we wanted our image's width and height to be 50% of `.intro`'s width and height, our rule would look like this:

```
.intro {
  background: url("bg-demo.jpg") no-repeat;
  background-size: 50% 50%;
}
```

As fun as `background-size` is, it's worth noting that older versions of Internet Explorer (versions 8 and lower) don't support it. If you're worried about fallbacks for those older browsers, I might suggest a variation on Paul Irish's conditional comments technique (http://bkaprt.com/rdpp/03-08/). In fact, you can see this in the HTML for http://responsivewebdesign.com/:

```
<!DOCTYPE html>
  <!--[if IE]><![endif]-->
  <!--[if lt IE 9]>  <html class="oldie ie">
  <![endif]-->
  <!--[if IE 9]>     <html class="ie ie9">
  <![endif]-->
  <!--[if gt IE 9]>  <html class="ie"><![endif]-->
  <!--[if !IE]><!--> <html> <!--<![endif]-->
```

With those conditional comments in place, older versions of IE will have a class of `oldie` applied to their opening `<html>` tag. As a result, I can apply an acceptable fallback style by starting a second selector with `.oldie`:

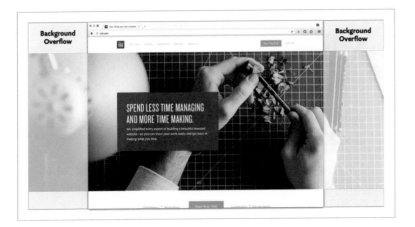

FIG 3.10: By using `background-size: cover`, the lead photo on Virb's responsive homepage proportionally resizes to, well, *cover* its container.

```
.intro {
  background: url("bg-demo.jpg") no-repeat;
  background-size: 50% 50%;
}
.oldie .intro {
  background-image: url("bg-demo-noresize.jpg");
}
```

With our fallbacks sorted, let's take a look at two incredibly useful keywords we can apply to the `background-size` property: `cover` and `contain`. Let's start with `cover`:

```
.intro {
  background: url("bg-demo.jpg") no-repeat;
  background-size: cover;
}
```

The browser will evaluate the width and height of the background image, and find the smaller of the two values. Once that's done, it will scale the image proportionally, ensuring that the smaller dimension—either the width or the height—covers

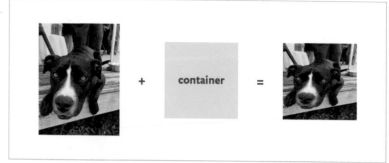

FIG 3.11: Need your background image to be completely visible *and* flexible? There's a `background-size: contain` for that.

its container. You can see this in action on Virb's responsive homepage (http://bkaprt.com/rdpp/03-09/). The lead image's native dimensions are `1600×600`. Since the height (600 pixels) is smaller than the width (1600 pixels), the image stretches vertically over the height of its container (**FIG 3.10**). No matter how large—or small!—that box becomes, the background scales proportionally to perfectly cover it.

Applying `background-size: contain` will also scale our backgrounds, but the resulting layout is quite different:

```
.intro {
  background: url("bg-demo.jpg") no-repeat;
  background-size: contain;
}
```

Whereas `background-size: cover` may occasionally hide parts of our images from view, `background-size: contain` ensures the entire background is always visible within its container (**FIG 3.11**).

When combined with `background-position`, `background-size` can create some really stunning image treatments. The

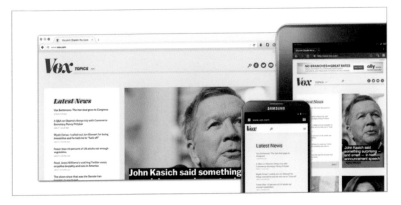

FIG 3.12: Vox's responsive homepage is a stunning combination of background images and lovingly typeset text (http://bkaprt.com/rdpp/03-10/).

homepage of Vox.com combines the two properties beautifully (**FIG 3.12**). Each of the blocks show featured stories and headlines with a flexible background image:

```
.content {
    background: url("beyonce_grammy.jpg") no-repeat;
    background-size: cover;
    background-position: center, center;
    height: 600px;
}
```

Rather than anchoring their images top and left within each block, Vox uses `background-position: center, center` to, well, center them within their containers (**FIG 3.13**). And with that positioning in place, `background-size: cover` ensures that each block is covered by a perfectly centered, flexible background.

In theory, Vox could use media queries to load different images at certain breakpoints, perhaps loading in widescreen-appropriate crops as the viewport expands:

```
.content {
  background: url("beyonce_grammy.jpg") no-repeat;
  background-size: cover;
  background-position: center, center;
  height: 600px;
}
@media screen and (min-width: 39em) {
  .content {
    background-image:
      url("beyonce_grammy-medium.jpg");
  }
}
@media screen and (min-width: 60em) {
  .content {
    background-image:
      url("beyonce_grammy-wide.jpg");
    background-position: 0 0;
  }
}
```

The sky is, as the kids say, the limit.

SCALING RESPONSIBLY: SRCSET AND SIZES

There are some very real downsides to simply scaling or shifting images with a bit of CSS. But thankfully, there are tools to help us tackle them. Let's step through each in turn.

First, CSS-based resizing can often be bad for the weight of our work. As of the middle of 2015, the average weight of a web page was 2.1MB (http://bkaprt.com/rdpp/03-11/), up from a relatively paltry 320KB in 2010 (http://bkaprt.com/rdpp/03-12/). And most of that weight? You guessed it: images. Our beloved JPGs, PNGs, and GIFs comprise more than 60% of that 2.1MB footprint—over 1.2MB per page on average.

Most of that has come about with high-density displays. In 2012, web developer Jason Grigsby found that the Apple.com homepage jumped in size from 500KB to well over 2 MB, simply by upgrading its images to higher-resolution versions that

FIG 3.13: By applying `background-size: cover` to their centered background images, Vox.com can feature content alongside rather evocative—and completely flexible—background images.

would look crisp on high-density screens (http://bkaprt.com/rdpp/03-13/). And Apple's not alone—as our screens have gotten sharper, our images have gotten bigger, bulking up our pages.

Given this ever-increasing page size, we should attend to the amount of data we're asking our users to download, rather than simply squishing down massive images to fit smaller screens. Now, to be clear: "small screen" does not imply "slow connection." Far from it. In fact, there is *no* correlation between the width of a screen and the amount of bandwidth available to it. My laptop could be tethered to a phone's 3G connection, on a steady ethernet connection, or on a hotel's barely-functioning Wi-Fi network; conversely, my phone could just as easily be on a fast, reliable Wi-Fi network as it could be connected to a flaky cellular signal. Right now, there's simply no way to detect the amount of bandwidth actually available to our users' devices.

To their credit, browser and hardware vendors are working on ways for us to detect a user's connection speed, like the

Network Information API (http://bkaprt.com/rdpp/03-14/), but a standard solution hasn't been established yet. In the short term, I think that uncertainty is actually okay. If anything, it emphasizes the need to reduce the amount of data we're serving to our users, regardless of the size of their screen. Jake Archibald, a developer advocate for Google Chrome, suggests that lower-end networks should be our true priority (http://bkaprt.com/rdpp/03-15/):

> It's important to focus on 3G load times, because even though we have 4G now, those users are on 3G (or worse) a lot of the time: a quarter of the time in the United States, half the time in large parts of Europe.

The commercial benefits of lighter pages are legion. GQ (http://bkaprt.com/rdpp/03-16/) recently found that its responsive redesign was entirely too slow—but by reducing page load time by 80%, its number of unique visitors jumped by 80% (http://bkaprt.com/rdpp/03-17/). If we assume *all* our users may have low bandwidth, it can help us lighten our sites and create interfaces that are fast for everyone—whether accessed on mobile, desktop, or something else entirely.

And that brings us back to flexible images. Those massive images can be resized to fit on smaller devices, but even if those tiny screens are on fast connections, they'll be downloading a lot of pixels they won't use. It's *invisible overhead,* and we should reduce it whenever possible. Thankfully, some standards-based tools are emerging to help us tackle this problem, authored by the Responsive Issues Community Group (http://bkaprt.com/rdpp/03-18/). They've worked with browser vendors to produce a number of additions to the HTML specification, specifically some attributes to make our images a bit more intelligent.

To begin, let's look at our dear friend, the humble img element:

```
<img src="img/main.jpg" alt="A friendly-looking dog"
   />
```

Nothing too fancy, right? Our img element has a src that points to the URL of an image file (img/main.jpg), accompanied by some accessible `alt` text to describe the contents of our image ("A friendly-looking dog"). And if we've done our job right, `main.jpg` should show up in our browser. But here's the thing: that image file is going to be served to every browser and device that accesses our page, regardless of its network speed, screen density, or viewport size.

To help our image scale more efficiently, we'll add one of the new responsive image tools: namely, the `srcset` attribute.

```
<img srcset="img/main-200.jpg 2x, img/main-300.jpg
    3x" src="img/main.jpg" alt="A friendly-looking
    dog" />
```

...okay, hold on a moment. Our once-pristine `img` element now looks like a Perl script threw up in the middle of our HTML. What, pray, is all that gibberish inside our `srcset` attribute? Commas? 2x? 3x? What is happening here?

Thankfully, it's not as bad as it looks. To decipher our `srcset` attribute, let's make it more legible:

```
<img srcset="img/retina.jpg 2x,
                img/retinarok.jpg 3x"
    src="img/normal.jpg" alt="A friendly-looking dog"
    />
```

That's a bit better. What we've done is create three different versions of our image, each identical, but with different *pixel densities:* their dimensions are the same, but they're tailored to be viewed on increasingly higher-resolution displays. And inside our `srcset`, we're simply spelling out the path to each image, and then describing its ideal pixel density—2x, 3x, and so on.

With those images and resolutions spelled out, our `img` tag is no longer loading one image for all screens: instead, our `srcset` is filled with *options* of multiple images that could be loaded, depending on which is best for the user. Armed with that information, the browser can select the image best suited to the density of the display. That prevents us from saddling

main-large.jpg   **main-medium.jpg**   **main-small.jpg**

FIG 3.14: Our three new images. Each of them is identical, except for their dimensions: they've simply been scaled down.

lower-resolution screens with incredibly complex images, and conserves some bandwidth in the process.

Neat, right? Unfortunately, those x descriptors are intended for *fixed-width* images, which are so, like, 1999. But all is not lost: we can use srcset to negotiate images based on the width available to them in the layout. Let's look at another img:

```
<img srcset="img/main-large.jpg 1440w,
  img/main-medium.jpg 720w, img/main-small.jpg 360w"
  src="img/main-medium.jpg" alt="A friendly-looking
  dog" />
```

And yep, once again, that looks a little terrifying. Sorry about that! Once you've climbed down from the flagpole, we can add a few well-placed line breaks, and produce something that looks a bit more sane:

```
<img srcset="img/main-large.jpg 1440w,
             img/main-medium.jpg 720w,
             img/main-small.jpg 360w"
     src="img/main-small.jpg" alt="A friendly-looking
     dog" />
```

As before, we've created three different versions of our image—but this time, they're each identical except for their scale: they only vary in size (FIG 3.14). Similarly, our srcset spells out the paths to each image, separated by commas. But this time, instead of using 2x or 3x modifiers to describe the density of the image, we're describing each image's width in pixels, followed by a w. Since main-large.jpg is 1440px wide, the 1440w allows us to tell the browser its native width. The same is true for our 720px-wide main-medium.jpg and our 360px-wide main-small.jpg—each is described as having widths of 720w and 360w, respectively.

(Quick aside: sharp readers will note that in both of our code snippets, there's still a src on our img elements. Strictly speaking, src is required by the responsive images specification—your images *must* have src attributes, even if you're using srcset (http://bkaprt.com/rdpp/03-19/). This might seem redundant, but is actually a boon for backwards compatibility. If a browser doesn't understand srcset, it'll still download an image.)

After specifying three different widths for the lead image, you might be wondering how we decide which image the browser loads. And that's a perfectly reasonable thing to wonder! But here's the thing: *we don't.* If you read the specification, there's nothing telling browsers how to "pick" the best option from srcset (http://bkaprt.com/rdpp/03-20/). It's up to the browser to choose the best image—not us.

...okay, I know how that sounds. Maybe you're mildly panicking. Maybe you're more-than-mildly panicking! After all, we're the designers! We should have the final say in which images our users see, right?

But really: don't worry. This lack of control is actually a good thing. Consider that these images aren't just chosen for which has the best "fit" for our layout: an image from srcset could be selected to match the speed of the user's network, the resolution of her display—or, or, *or*. There are countless factors that determine which image is the best pick. And while some things in our responsive images toolkit allow us a higher degree of control, determining the best *resolution* for our image is best left to the browser. It'll keep our markup lighter, and our users happier.

While we can't choose the best option out of `srcset`, we can help the browser make a more intelligent selection. To do that, we'll add a `sizes` attribute:

```
<img srcset="img/main-large.jpg 1440w,
             img/main-medium.jpg 720w,
             img/main-small.jpg 360w"
  sizes="(min-width: 50em) 250px,
         (min-width: 35em) 33vw,
         100vw"
  src="img/main-medium.jpg" alt="A friendly-looking
    dog" />
```

So again, I realize that (`min-width: 50em`) `250px`, (`min-width: 35em`) `33vw`, `100vw` looks a lot like unadulter-ated, robot-generated gobbledygook. But as with `srcset`, we're creating a list of items our browser, each separated by a comma. Basically, each entry in our list describes the physical width of our image at different points in our responsive design—that is to say, the *size* it will occupy in the layout.

Let's walk through our `sizes` attribute, and see if we can't decipher it:

1. (`min-width: 50em`) `250px` looks a little like a media query, doesn't it? In fact, that's basically what it is: we're telling the browser that if the viewport has a minimum width of `50em`, the image will be `250px` wide.
2. (`min-width: 35em`) `33vw` works basically the same way: if the viewport has a minimum width of `35em`, the image will be `33vw` in width. But what's a `vw`, you ask? Well, a `vw` is just another unit of length in CSS, equal to 1% of the view-

port's width. So `33vw` is another way of saying the image will occupy 33% of the width of the viewport.

3. `100vw` is the default value for the `sizes` attribute. It means the image will occupy the full width of the viewport. So if the condition in our first `sizes` entry isn't met—that is, if our viewport is below that `min-width: 40em` threshold—then our image will be sized at 100% of the viewport's width.

The sizes listed in our, um, `sizes` attribute don't need to perfectly match the image's size at each breakpoint. What we're trying to capture is an *approximation* of the image's width as the layout changes. Once it's armed with information about how an image will be laid out, the browser can intelligently select an image from our `srcset` list and pick the best possible option to load.

(Quick tip: if you're a fan of valid HTML, the `sizes` attribute is actually required by the specification. In other words, if you use `srcset`, it should be accompanied by a corresponding `sizes`. At the time of this writing, `srcset` will still *work* without `sizes`, but it'll make your markup invalid. So tread carefully.)

A note about support, before we continue:

- A number of non-desktop browsers offer fair support for `srcset` and `sizes`. On both iOS and Mac OS X, Safari has partial support for the two attributes. It supports resolution switching with the `x` descriptor, but not with `w`. Newer default browsers for Android—including Chrome and the default Android browser—support the attributes handily.

  However, it's not all good news: neither Android's default browser (as of Android 4.4.4) nor Opera Mini (as of version 8, at least) support `srcset` or `sizes`. Nor do they natively support any other part of the responsive images specification—and that's unfortunate for us, as both of these browsers are massively popular.

- In happier news, support for `srcset` and `sizes` is fairly robust among most modern desktop browsers. Chrome, for example, has supported `srcset` and `sizes` since version 38, while Opera has supported it since version 26. At the time of this writing, Firefox is still finalizing its implementation of `srcset` and `sizes`, but allows you to activate the attributes if you root around in the developer preferences. And while Internet Explorer hasn't shipped a working version, it is actively working on support for the new attributes (http:// bkaprt.com/rdpp/03-21/).

Overall, the support for responsive images is impressive, but still in its infancy—a significant number of browsers don't yet support `srcset` or `sizes` natively. However, you can use a JavaScript library like Picturefill (http://bkaprt.com/rdpp/03-22/) to patch responsive image support into older browsers. Simply download Picturefill into your project, and include the following in the `head` of your document:

```
<script>document.createElement( "picture" );</script>
<script src="/path/to/picturefill.js" async></script>
```

And with that, you'll have responsive images working seamlessly in your flexible layouts, *responsibly* resizing with a little help from `srcset` and `sizes`.

But watch your step, dear reader: while `srcset` and `sizes` can make CSS-resized images a little more weight-conscious, sometimes scaling an image with CSS isn't ideal. In some cases, flexible images can harm more than they help.

When resizing brings regret

...okay, I apologize for the dire note. There's nothing *wrong* with a little `max-width: 100%` to make your `img` elements more flexible—and what's more, it'll work perfectly for most of your images. But sometimes, simply scaling images up or down can reduce their clarity.

Here's a quick example: open "What is Paul Krugman Afraid Of?" (http://bkaprt.com/rdpp/03-23/) on a reasonably large screen, say, a laptop or a tablet. Throughout the interview, you'll notice several photos with text overlaid on them (**FIG 3.15**). Now, there are a number of potential accessibility issues

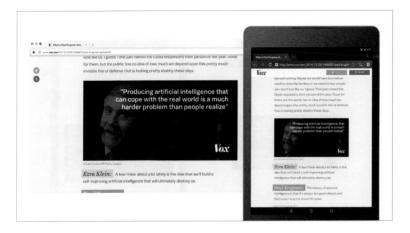

FIG 3.15: Vox features quite lovely visual pull quotes, with text overlaid atop images.

in typesetting pull quotes in images—they'd need `alt` attributes to be accessible to non-sighted readers—but let's put those aside for a moment, and focus on the responsive layout alone.

Since the article's layout is responsive, Vox used `max-width: 100%` to ensure that as their flexible grid reshapes itself, the images never break out of their containing elements. Because of that, opening the same article on a smaller screen resizes the images, but the pull quotes are considerably less legible than on wider screens (**FIG 3.16**).

This is equally true on complex images and charts, if not more so. For example, take the map near the top of this page on Columbia's School of Engineering site (http://bkaprt.com/rdpp/03-24/; **FIG 3.17**). In addition to the colored blocks representing energy consumption across New York City neighborhoods, there's the title of the graph, a legend to help you decipher the map, pie charts for specific land areas, and so on. The image is, in other words, incredibly dense. So while it could be resized, all of those finer details would be lost, and the meaning of the image would degrade.

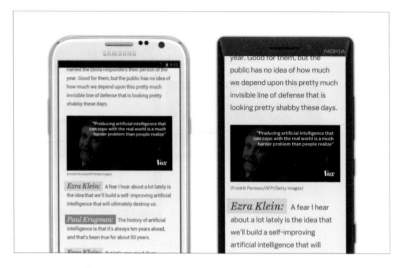

FIG 3.16: On smaller screens, simply resizing the images makes their text hard to read. Flexible, but frustrating.

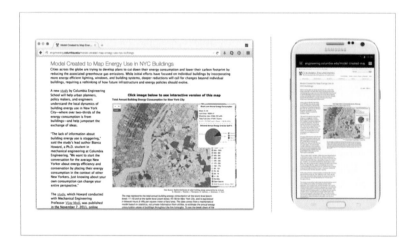

FIG 3.17: A useful and interactive map of New York. Is there a way to effectively resize something this dense?

The form, frame, and shape of our images

The problem with CSS-based resizing is that it's *content-blind:* it focuses on the shape of the container that holds the image, not the image itself. And sometimes, if we're not paying attention, those images can be resized past the point of usefulness.

This isn't a new problem. Long before the advent of the web, photographers and graphic designers have been concerned with resizing their work effectively, and how to preserve the integrity of their artwork across differently-sized media. In the middle of the twentieth century, the Swiss designer Karl Gerstner applied a systematic approach to the problem, demonstrating how a design system could be used to adapt a wordmark so that it doesn't just fit in different paper formats, it *thrives* (**FIG 3.18**).

More recently, designer Raymond Brigleb charted the rise of the cassette tape's popularity in the '80s and the challenge it posed for the designers of LP album covers. Constrained by the cassette's smaller size and unforgivingly weird aspect ratio, designers changed the layout, size, and position of key elements to preserve the message they wanted to convey (**FIG 3.19**).

Even the process of cropping a photograph relies on understanding the contents of the picture, not simply its dimensions. A photographer identifies the primary subject of a photograph—the focal point—and trims away the inessential parts of the picture. Various crops of a photograph may differ greatly in the amount of detail shown, but the subject is usually consistent. As different as they might look, all of the crops are, in essence, the same photo (**FIG 3.20**).

In looking at the problem of making our images not just resize, but *respond,* there have been some attempts to automate intelligent image cropping. For example, Adam Bradley built a framework that allowed designers to apply CSS classes to an image's container that would, in turn, preserve the focal point as the image scaled up or down (http://bkaprt.com/rdpp/03-25/).

So it's absolutely possible—and often ideal—to simply resize your images with a mixture of `max-width: 100%`, `srcset`, and `sizes`. But it's worth remembering that the images inside our documents are actually documents themselves. After all,

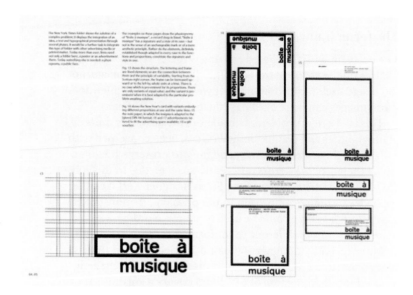

FIG 3.18: In his book *Designing Programmes,* Karl Gerstner demonstrated how a well-thought-out design system could maintain a logo's integrity on any number of printed formats, from full-sized advertisements to handheld gift cards (http://bkaprt.com/rdpp/03-26/).

they're there to convey information to our readers, so we should ensure the message survives at any scale.

FINER-GRAINED CONTROL: PICTURE AND SOURCE

In other words, you might come across situations when images shouldn't be resized, but *replaced*—swapped for alternate files optimized for different breakpoints, ensuring that they maintain clarity even as their containers expand and contract. When that happens, you'll want to specify a completely different image to load.

The Cassette Tape as
Responsive Design

When I was growing up, my favorite medium for art was the music album. And while the LP Record was the "fine art" of the category, the humble cassette tape was too convenient to ignore. For most of the Eighties, that's how I bought my music.

But this format was frustrating to someone who cared about the artwork and design. The usable space went from 144 square inches to a mere 10, and the aspect ratio changed completely. It was inevitable that the layout would have to change, too.

FIG 3.19: In reviewing how album cover art had to adapt across LPs and cassettes, Raymond Brigleb demonstrates the need for responsive images (http://bkaprt.com/rdpp/03-27/). (And suggests, I think, that our problems on the web aren't entirely new.)

FIG 3.20: While the dimensions of a photograph may change from crop to crop, the focal point remains intact. Photograph by Tim Evanson (http://bkaprt.com/rdpp/03-28/).

Of course, that's just for background images. Inline images, such as those specified by our industrious img element, need some extra help. And that's where the new picture element comes in. As it happens, Shopify's responsive site has a great example of picture in action. Near the top of their homepage is a photo of a Shopify customer, which is repositioned at different breakpoints (**FIG 3.21**). But if you look under the hood, you'll see that it's not one photo, but three—each sized and cropped slightly differently from the others (**FIG 3.22**). And if

FIG 3.21: Follow the photo: the lead picture on Shopify's responsive homepage is repositioned at different breakpoints (http://bkaprt.com/rdpp/03-29/).

homepage-person@desktop.png   homepage-person@tablet.png   homepage-person@mobile.png

FIG 3.22: It might look like one image, but it's actually *three:* each photo features the same subject, but with a slightly different crop.

you look at the page's source, you'll see our first example of the `picture` element:

```
<picture>
  <source
    srcset="homepage-person@desktop.png"
    media="(min-width: 990px)">
  <source
    srcset="homepage-person@tablet.png"
    media="(min-width: 750px)">
  <img
    srcset="homepage-person@mobile.png"
    alt="A featured Shopify Merchant">
</picture>
```

I've simplified their markup slightly, but the structure's the same. As you can see, a `picture` element contains any number of `source` elements, and exactly one `img`. On each `source`, there's a media query inside the oh-so-aptly named `media` attribute. The browser loops through each of the `source` elements until it finds one whose media query matches the conditions in the browser. Upon finding a match, it will send that `source`'s `srcset` to the `img` element and load it.

And that relationship between the `source` and the `img` is actually quite important: the matching `source` is never rendered by the browser. In fact, neither is the `picture` element: the `srcset` of the relevant `source` element is sent to the innermost `img`, and *that's* what gets displayed. So on widescreen displays, the `source` with (`min-width: 990px`) will send the largest version of Shopify's lead photo to the `img`; on midsize breakpoints, `homepage-person@tablet.png` will get rendered, thanks to the (`min-width: 750px`) query. And finally, if *none* of the media queries match, the browser will just load the `img`.

Instead of using `srcset` and `sizes` to load bigger and smaller versions of the same image, `picture` allows us to tailor our image content to fit specific viewports. In the language of the responsive images specification, this is referred to as *art direction*. Rather than simply resizing the image, we're cropping or otherwise optimizing it to fit a specific breakpoint. In doing so, we're ensuring that it still conveys its meaning, even though the details inside the image may change.

But swapping in different crops of images isn't all the `picture` element can do. In fact, take a quick look at http://responsivewebdesign.com/workshop. Halfway down the page, you'll see a list of logos (**FIG 3.23**). If you peek under the hood, each of those logos look something like this:

```
<picture>
  <source srcset="/logos/cibc.svg"
    type="image/svg+xml" />
  <img src="/logos/cibc.png" alt="CIBC" />
</picture>
```

FIG 3.23: A little list of logos, powered by picture.

You might have noticed our `picture` element is completely lacking in media queries. Instead, there's a single `type` attribute on the `source`, indicating that the image it references is actually a vector-based SVG file (`image/svg+xml`). So instead of using media queries to select an image, our browser is actually checking our `sources` to see if it supports their individual `types`. In this particular case, we're looking for SVG support: if a browser supports that `image/svg+xml` format, then it'll load the vector-based version of the image; but if it doesn't, it'll just load the PNG specified in our `img`.

In theory, we could extend this further, enhancing our `srcset` with some of those resolution-sensitive `w` or `x` flags we discussed earlier. This `type`-based switching allows us to use the `picture` element to ask a browser which file formats it supports. And it gets considerably more powerful when coupled with media queries, as you'll see if you look at the logo at the top of the Responsive Web Design site (http://responsivewebdesign.com/workshop):

```
<picture>
  <source
    media="(min-width: 50em)"
    type="image/svg+xml"
    srcset="/img/logo-rwd-sq.svg" />
  <source
    media="(min-width: 50em)"
    srcset="/img/logo-rwd-sq.png" />
  <source
    media="(min-width: 39em)"
    type="image/svg+xml"
    srcset="/img/logo-rwd.svg" />
  <source
    media="(min-width: 39em)"
    srcset="/img/logo-rwd.png" />
  <source
    type="image/svg+xml"
    srcset="/img/logo-rwd-sq.svg" />
  <img src="/img/logo-rwd-sq.png" alt="Responsive
    Web Design" />
</picture>
```

Here we're combining media queries on each `source` with a `type` attribute, allowing us to query not just the width of the viewport, but whether or not the browser *also* supports SVG (`type="image/svg+xml"`). And we're doing so at multiple breakpoints. At the widest ((`min-width: 50em`)) and smallest ends of the masthead's layout, we're looking to load a two-line version of the image, either as a SVG (`logo-rwd.svg`) or PNG (`logo-rwd.svg`). But at the middle breakpoint ((`min-width: 39em`)), the wordmark's laid out in a single line; and once again, we're using `type`-based switching to test for SVG support.

All that extra code might look complex, but the process is still the same: our browser is going to start at the top of our `source`s, and work its way down, searching for a `source` whose media query matches the viewport *and* whose `type` attribute matches the image formats supported by the browser. Once it finds a match, it'll send that `srcset` to the `img` to be rendered; if there aren't any matches, then it'll just load our `img`.

DESIGNER, FRAME THYSELF

We've looked at an incredibly broad array of techniques in this chapter. But in many ways, we're being asked to balance our designerly need for control—using `background-position` and `background-size` in our CSS, or `picture` in our markup—with the browser's ability to solve some of these image problems for us with `srcset` and `sizes`. More than any coding technique, that feels like the biggest challenge: to reframe the discussion to focus not on a specific technology, but on relinquishing perfect control over the experience.

4 RESPONSIVE ADVERTISING

FOR ALMOST AS LONG AS we've printed on paper, we've had advertising. Longer, even: campaign slogans and advertisements have been discovered on the walls of Pompeii. In ancient Egypt, papyrus was often pounded into sales messages and hung prominently. But once we figured out that whole "paper" thing, advertising *really* took off. The earliest printed advertisement is a handbill for wares from tenth-century China (**FIG 4.1**).

I'm sure the advertisements with which you're most familiar are from the printed page—specifically, the display ads that appear in magazines, newspapers, and other periodicals. But those began modestly. Take a look at the first known advertisement for coffee, which appeared in the pages of the *Publick Adviser* in the seventeenth century (**FIG 4.2**). It was a text-only affair, featuring an understated (and rather poetic) testimonial for a roaster's services. A century later, if you were to squint at the front page of the Times of London, you might notice ads for shipping merchants nestled among the columns (**FIG 4.3**). But over time, of course, printed display ads evolved beyond their humble beginnings to become more, well, flamboyant in nature (**FIG 4.4**).

FIG 4.1: From stone walls to handbills, from papyrus to newsprint, advertising's been around for some time. (http://bkaprt.com/rdpp/04-01/; http://bkaprt.com/rdpp/04-02/; http://bkaprt.com/rdpp/04-03/)

FIG 4.2: In its earliest days, advertising often preferred prose to pictures, as seen in London's *Publick Adviser* (http://bkaprt. com/rdpp/04-04/; http://bkaprt.com/ rdpp/04-05/).

FIG 4.3: Other than some visual ornaments and slightly more adventurous typesetting, display advertisements still feel fairly understated a century later (http://bkaprt. com/rdpp/04-06/).

FIG 4.4: Of course, ads got a little more … vivid over time. (http://bkaprt.com/rdpp/04-07/; http://bkaprt.com/rdpp/04-08/; http://bkaprt.com/rdpp/04-09/; http://bkaprt.com/rdpp/04-10/; http://bkaprt.com/rdpp/04-11/)

When the web came along, it's only natural that we borrowed the advertising practices that seemed to work for print-based publishers. The trajectory for digital ads was, in many ways, similar to print. From simple, modest banners to the complex interactive ads of today, the design of digital advertising has evolved into its own distinct practice (**FIG 4.5–4.6**). For good or ill, much of our medium is supported by advertising—and this presents a unique challenge for responsive layouts. Because when it comes to responsive design, digital advertising is one of the elephants in the room: after all, most ads on the web are fixed-width.

I know, I'm as shocked as you are. But it's true! Take, for example, the Interactive Advertising Bureau (IAB), the consortium responsible for defining most standards for online advertising. If you read their guidelines for desktop (http://bkaprt.com/rdpp/04-12/) or mobile (http://bkaprt.com/rdpp/04-13/), you'll see that each entry in the list—the 300×250 "medium rect-

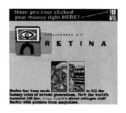

FIG 4.5: Love them or loathe them, these early banner ads from O'Reilly and HotWired helped kickstart the digital advertising industry—and, eventually, the rise of ad blockers.

FIG 4.6: Banners, videos, and rollovers—oh my!

FIG 4.7: You can have ads in any shape you want. (As long as you like pixels.)

angle" ad, the 160×600 "skyscraper" ad, and so on—has a specific width and height, defined in perfectly inflexible pixels (**FIG 4.7**).

I mention this not because I hate pixels. (Much.) But this presents a challenge to responsive designers. Though our layouts have become more flexible, responsive, and device-agnostic, most standard advertisement sizes are still defined in specific, fixed dimensions. So, how are we supposed to incorporate them into decidedly fluid designs?

I'll jump to the punchline: there's no perfect answer quite yet. Responsive advertising is still very much a work in progress, but there are a number of emerging patterns we can use. Let's take a look.

(Hang on: aren't punchlines supposed to be funny?)

CONDITIONAL LOADING

Smashing Magazine, an online publication for web designers and developers, launched a striking new responsive site in 2012 (**FIG 4.8**). Featuring an airy palette alongside considered, elegant typography, the Elliott Jay Stocks-designed site is a joy to read

FIG 4.8: *Smashing Magazine,* sporting a stately responsive design.

on any device. If your browser is on a reasonably wide display, you'll see a fair number of advertisements within the fixed-width sidebar on the right side of the screen. But if you open the site on a smaller display—like a phone or small tablet—the ads aren't visible. Below a certain point, they're completely hidden.

Here's a quick look at the CSS that creates the effect:

```
.sb {
  display: none;
}
@media screen and (min-width: 63.75em) {
  .sb {
    display: block;
  }
}
```

The block that contains the advertisements—a div with a class of .sb—is set to display: none by default. But above a view-port width of 63.75em, or approximately 1020px, the sidebar's

FIG 4.9: *Smashing*'s ads are hidden from view, but still loaded.

`display` property is set to `block`, allowing it to reappear on the right edge of the design, ads triumphantly in view.

Seems like a reasonable approach, no? After all, below a certain width, the ads would be incredibly difficult to integrate into the responsive layout. But if you poke around in your browser's inspector, you'll see the ads are still loaded: the code to display and download the ads still runs (**FIG 4.9**). There are simply a few lines of CSS to hide them from view.

There are a number of challenges with hiding content when it doesn't fit. From an advertising standpoint, this might mean widescreen readers are subsidizing the experience for those on smaller displays. (Assuming, of course, that hidden ads aren't counted as "viewed" by their advertisers.) And as we discussed before, extra (but hidden) code can introduce needless overhead into our designs. If a certain class of users—mobile, tablet, desktop, or otherwise—won't benefit from a certain piece of content, simply hiding that information with CSS adds extra weight to the page that won't benefit the reader.

Beyond the ads themselves, there are other potentially important pieces of content within that sidebar—a number of

FIG 4.10: It's not just ads: there are other pieces of great content hidden from small screens.

promotional blurbs for various books, a newsletter subscription form, and so on—that are hidden from smaller screens (**FIG 4.10**). These are, I hasten to add, not criticisms of *Smashing Magazine:* hiding content that "doesn't fit" is a common technique on many responsive sites. But whether we're designing text, video, imagery, or advertising, we should be looking for opportunities to *simplify* our designs, rather than *suppressing* information. A better approach would be to load only what we need at any given viewport, rather than hiding the excess with CSS. More specifically, we can start by identifying the ads best suited for each breakpoint, and then load them only if the design can accommodate them.

Back in Chapter 2, we took a brief look at responsive navigation that used conditional loading to *(ahem)* load more complex menus conditionally: say, when a viewport was above a certain width. Currently, the markup for the sidebar element—our `.sb` div—is included directly in the page, and hidden with CSS:

```
<div class="sb">
  <!-- Code for sidebar -->
  …
</div>
```

In theory, we could use the Ajax-Include pattern (http://bkaprt.com/rdpp/02-08/) to load the markup for the sidebar conditionally, by removing the content and moving it to an external file—say, `sidebar-contents.html`:

```
<div class="sb"
  data-append="/include/sidebar-contents.html"
  data-media="(min-width: 63.75em)"></div>
```

This is only a sketch, but it shows how the Ajax-Include pattern might work. The `data-append` attribute points to the URL of our snippet, which contains the content to be appended to the `div`; `data-media`, however, says the snippet should be loaded *if* our viewport is `63.75em` or wider. Otherwise, if the viewport is smaller than that threshold, the `div` remains empty.

FIG 4.11: Ads may appear underneath the lead stories on smaller screens.

RETHINKING THE HIERARCHY

While redesigning their site in 2011, the *Boston Globe* came up with a pattern to address their responsive advertising problem: namely, that the placement of an advertisement would be determined by the width of the page. When the site was a single column, ads could be inserted into sensible points in the content flow. A large ad might appear immediately after the lead stories on the homepage—but only on narrower screens (**FIG 4.11**). As the layout widened to two columns, the ad would move from its initial position and stick to the top of that new column. Similarly, when a third column appeared at the widest breakpoint, the ad would shift again (**FIG 4.12–13**).

I was part of the team working on the redesign, and we all felt the *Globe's* suggested pattern was a downright novel approach to making their ads responsive. However, it did require a slight departure from their traditional method of inserting ads into pages. Historically, producers would insert some JavaScript in a page's HTML, like so:

```
<script>insertAd( 'MAIN_AD' );</script>
```

FIG 4.12: At a wider breakpoint, the ad's promoted to the second column.

FIG 4.13: As the design gets wider still, the ad moves to the third column.

It looks fairly straightforward, because it's designed to be: the `insertAd()` function is tasked with inserting an ad of some type (specifically, `MAIN_AD`) at that specific point in the layout. But that simplicity's short-lived. Once that code is run by the browser, it often turns into complex-looking JavaScript—specifically, a series of `document.write()` statements:

```
<script>
document.write( »
  '<script src="ad-load.js"></script>' );
document.write( »
  '<style>.ad { border: 1px solid; … }</style>' );
…
</script>
```

It's a bit more complicated, but the spirit's the same: those `document.write()` statements are responsible for inserting the `MAIN_AD` advertisement into the design, along with any JavaScript and CSS files it requires. This inline approach is very common on the web, and it definitely got points for reliability, because you knew exactly where each ad would be placed. But unfortunately, it doesn't work for a more responsive solution like the one outlined by the *Globe,* in which an ad could appear in multiple potential locations.

Complicating matters is `document.write()` itself. First of all, it's terrible for performance: while the browser downloads all the external images, styles, and assets required to render the ad, any content on the page after those `document.write()` statements is prevented from loading (**FIG 4.14**). The effect on the user's experience can be terrible, especially on lower-powered devices or slower networks. What's more, once content's been written into the page with `document.write()`, it can't be moved around with JavaScript. If we had used this method, our ad would have been locked into place, making `document.write()`-generated content incompatible with our responsive advertising pattern.

To make our ads responsive-friendly, our first step was to remove all inline JavaScript. Instead, we looked at all the areas where ads could *potentially* appear—underneath the lead stories, at the top of the block for the second column, and then at the top of the third column—and inserted an empty `div` into each location:

```
<div data-adname="MAIN_AD" class="ad-slot-a"></div>
…
<div data-adname="MAIN_AD" class="ad-slot-b"></div>
```

FIG 4.14: `document.write()`: great for inserting content at a precise point in the design; not so great at performance.

```
...
<div data-adname="MAIN_AD" class="ad-slot-c"></div>
```

While each `div` is completely empty, it does have two pieces of descriptive information attached to it. The first is `data-adname`, an HTML5 `data-` attribute, which contains the name of the ad it will eventually contain. (I am, like, a genius at naming things.) The other snippet of metadata is a humble `class` attribute, which allows us to distinguish each ad container from its siblings.

Pretty modest markup, but this was the foundation for our responsive advertising pattern. In the examples below, we'll be using a `class` attribute as a kind of "hook" to apply simple styles—namely, by selectively hiding or showing each block at different breakpoints. With that `display` toggle in place, we can write some light JavaScript to not just insert the ads, but to shuttle them from one position to the next:

1. The script begins by looping through all `divs` that share a `data-adname` value, and looking for the first one that's set to `display: block`.
2. Once it's found, our JavaScript inserts the ad into that slot.
3. Whenever the browser window resizes or the device's orientation changes, the JavaScript starts the process over again: looking for the visible block, and moving the ad into that container.

By only showing one container at each layout breakpoint, our JavaScript can place the ad into the appropriate container, making our ads breakpoint-sensitive. We begin by showing only the ad block that appears immediately after the lead stories—that is, the container with a `class` of `ad-slot-a`:

```
.ad-slot-a {
  display: block;
}
.ad-slot-b,
.ad-slot-c {
  display: none;
}
```

We've hidden `ad-slot-b` and `ad-slot-c` from view, so our JavaScript loops through all of the `MAIN_AD` containers, and sees that only `ad-slot-a` is visible. And since the `div` is set to `display: block`, our script inserts the ad into that container, like so:

```
<div data-adname="MAIN_AD" class="ad-slot-a">
  <a class="ad" href="http://example.com/">
    <img src="http://example.com/ad-main.gif"
      alt="" />
  </a>
</div>
  …
```

```
<div data-adname="MAIN_AD" class="ad-slot-b"></div>

...

<div data-adname="MAIN_AD" class="ad-slot-c"></div>
```

Once our viewport gets a little wider—around `30em`—the second column becomes available. At that point, we'll update our CSS slightly to *only* show `ad-slot-b`, the second of our three ad containers:

```
@media (min-width: 30em) {
  .ad-slot-b {
    display: block;
  }
  .ad-slot-a,
  .ad-slot-c {
    display: none;
  }
}
```

With `ad-slot-a` hidden, our JavaScript runs again, and notices that `ad-slot-b` is visible. As a result, our script inserts the ad into that container:

```
<div data-adname="MAIN_AD" class="ad-slot-a"></div>

...

<div data-adname="MAIN_AD" class="ad-slot-b">
  <a class="ad" href="http://example.com/">
    <img src="http://example.com/ad-main.gif"
      alt="" />
  </a>
</div>

...

<div data-adname="MAIN_AD" class="ad-slot-c"></div>
```

Then, at the widest breakpoint, we could hide all of our containers, *except* the one atop the rightmost column—`ad-slot-c`:

```
@media (min-width: 50em) {
  .ad-slot-c {
    display: block;
  }
  .ad-slot-a,
  .ad-slot-b {
    display: none;
  }
}
```

With these two simple rules in place, our JavaScript will—you guessed it—move the ad into our third and final container:

```
<div data-adname="MAIN_AD" class="ad-slot-a"></div>
…
<div data-adname="MAIN_AD" class="ad-slot-b"></div>
…
<div data-adname="MAIN_AD" class="ad-slot-c">
  <a class="ad" href="http://example.com/">
    <img src="http://example.com/ad-main.gif"
      alt="" />
  </a>
</div>
```

With our modest CSS toggle and some lightweight JavaScript, our ad is finally getting a properly responsive treatment (**FIG 4.15**). It's never resized or clipped, but it is repositioned to maintain its visibility and make the best use of the space available. This approach isn't limited to the *Boston Globe*'s responsive design. In fact, this pattern evolved into Filament Group's AppendAround library (http://bkaprt.com/rdpp/04-15/), which allows responsively-minded designers to shuttle any content—not just advertisements—from one container to another.

Repositioning advertisements within a responsive design is quickly becoming a standard for many publishers. Several of Vox Media's responsive sites, including Vox.com, have adopted this pattern (**FIG 4.16**). Their approach, however, is slightly different. According to Jesse Young, a member of Vox Media's

FIG 4.15: Lightweight JavaScript and CSS, combined to shuttle an ad around the page.

FIG 4.16: Vox Media rotates content responsively around the ad, not the other way around.

product team, they've elected to move not the ads, but everything else (http://bkaprt.com/rdpp/04-16/):

> Ad placement is slightly trickier. We may want the banner to appear only on the right side of the screen and nowhere else. To ensure this, we use JavaScript for repositioning. However, it's worth noting that we don't actually reposition the ad but the content around it, instead. Because once an ad has rendered, performing DOM manipulation directly on it creates unwanted behaviors like creating tracking inaccuracies or causing the ad to disappear.

Here's the thing, though: when it comes to responsive advertising, layout is the easy part. In many ways, we've got bigger challenges ahead.

A NEED FOR NEW MODELS

Some time ago, designer Mark Boulton took a step back from problems of layout, and described a number of the deeper challenges with making our advertising responsive (http://bkaprt.com/rdpp/04-17/):

> Here's the problem as I see it:
> - A large number of sites rely on advertising for revenue. Many of those sites will benefit from a responsive web design approach.
> - Web advertising is a whole other industry.
> - Ad units are fixed, standardised sizes.
> - They are commissioned, sold and created on the basis of their size and position on the page
> - Many ads are rich (including takeovers, video, pop-overs, flyouts and interactions)

We've already discussed some of the layout problems, including that advertisements are fixed and inflexible, and aren't usable across various device classes and screen sizes. But Boulton gets to the root of some deeper, business-related issues—namely, the advertising industry operates independently from the rest of the web, and still considers the sale of digital ads in print-centric, position-specific terms.

In a pair of essays on the topic, designer and art director Roger Black approached the problem from another standpoint—namely, that the *business* of online advertising is far from ready for the web's multi-device nature (http://bkaprt. com/rdpp/04-18/, http://bkaprt.com/rdpp/04-19/):

> *Web, tablet and mobiles are sold and served separately, and there are not analytics services that can yet follow a multi-platform campaign. Right now the only way to get responsive advertising is a custom sell, and custom creative...[T]here is no single way to buy and insert adaptive ads across the platforms. The Interactive Advertising Bureau, which has worked over the years to promote standard sizes for ads for the desktop web, doesn't even list mobile ad sizes with its web ad units.*

Black was writing about the problem in 2011, but the underlying issues haven't changed much. Many advertising networks still think of "mobile," "tablet," and "desktop" as distinct products to be managed and sold, making it difficult for companies to coordinate ad campaigns across multiple device types. This problem will only get more complicated over time, of course—soon, "mobile," "tablet," and "desktop" won't be the only categories we're designing for. (And they shouldn't be.) According to research published by Google, this siloed approach desperately needs to catch up with our multiscreen reality (http://bkaprt. com/rdpp/04-20/). People rarely begin and end a particular workflow on one device; instead, we might begin shopping on our phones, before completing the checkout on our tablets or laptops.

Like our responsive layouts, our ads need to become not just more fluid in shape, but also in delivery. And while the advertising industry has yet to modernize their layout standards or business practices, many organizations have opted to try and fix responsive advertising internally, by designing and developing custom-built, more flexible ad formats in-house (**FIG 4.17**). According to Vox Media's Trei Brundrett, this approach didn't

FIG 4.17: Many publishers, like the *Boston Globe,* have been bucking industry standards and started designing flexible advertisements in-house.

just yield more responsive-friendly ads for their websites—it created ads that were less intrusive *and* more profitable (http://bkaprt.com/rdpp/04-21/):

> Our guiding principle is that advertising is part of the total user experience…It turns out that a great user experience with your advertising integrated with what you're building, your advertising performs better. It performs better for everybody.

There's something appealing about that formula. Rather than seeing digital advertising as somehow incompatible with an elegant, reader-friendly design, publishers are suggesting that flexible, responsive-friendly ads result in happier advertisers *and* readers.

The digital advertising team at the *Guardian* describes their cross-device advertising experiments in similar terms, saying their new responsive ad units are "better for advertisers, better for the *Guardian* and better for our readers" (http://bkaprt.com/rdpp/04-23/). Since their site sees a massive amount of diversity in screen sizes and device classes each month—"6000 different types [and] counting"—the *Guardian* created a few flexible versions of standard ad sizes (**FIG 4.18**). To do so, they broke each

FIG 4.18: Absent an industry standard, the *Guardian* created a number of responsive ad units in-house (http://bkaprt.com/rdpp/04-22/).

advertisement into its component parts, and treated them like a small-scale responsive design:

> To build this unit, we abstracted the various elements of an advert: the background, the subject image, the branding and the call to action. These are then populated individually into the HTML5 ad unit to allow the unit to respond best to the space available.

By treating their advertisements as small-scale responsive layouts instead of fixed, inflexible blocks, publishers like the *Guardian* are able to reposition these elements within a flexible, responsive canvas.

Of course, not every site has the resources to design their own responsive-friendly ad formats and sell them to prospective advertisers. Thankfully, Monotype has built demos of various responsive ad formats with lightweight, standards-based technologies—each one designed for flexibility from the outset (**FIG 4.19**). And Google—that scrappy little search engine—has released a responsive unit for its AdSense advertising service,

FIG 4.19: Monotype's various responsive ad formats are wonderful proofs-of-concept (http://bkaprt.com/rdpp/04-24/).

which should help make responsive advertising more broadly accessible (http://bkaprt.com/rdpp/04-25/).

Responsive advertising is still very much in its early days. As of this writing, the advertising industry hasn't made much progress on truly cross-device advertising, focusing instead on contractual language to improve ad visibility, and investing heavily on designing distinct ad formats for "mobile" and "desktop" (http://bkaprt.com/rdpp/04-26/). And publishers are painfully aware of this gap, as Peter Bale, CNN International Digital's vice president, noted recently (http://bkaprt.com/rdpp/04-27/):

> The ad industry has not fully come down the pipe yet in terms of responsively designed ads that will particularly work to the same level of monetisation on any device—there is a lag there. We have to move ahead of that and that's very difficult.

Until that "lag" disappears, it seems it's up to us to address user-facing issues like performance or layout—and to come up with our own ways of making advertising lightweight, flexible, and responsive.

5 DESIGNING THE INFINITE GRID

> *" What works is better than what looks good.*
> *The* looks good *can change, but what works, works."*
> **—RAY EAMES**

THE PAST FEW CHAPTERS have probably felt a bit like we've been sitting at a microscope. We've been taking close looks at the more challenging *components* of a responsive design, and discussing common principles for dealing with navigation, images, and advertising. But no element of your design exists in isolation. There comes a time when these small layout systems need to be stitched together into something larger—something flexible, responsive, and—hopefully—beautiful.

This book began with a quote by Trent Walton, one I thought it'd be helpful to return to (http://bkaprt.com/rdpp/05-01/):

> *I traded the control I had in Photoshop for a new kind of control—using flexible grids, flexible images, and media queries to build not a page, but a network of content that can be rearranged at any screen size to best convey a message.*

"A network of content"—such a lovely image, that. But while we've been focusing on the discrete components of our responsive layouts—the content—it's important that we not lose sight of the other half of that phrase: the larger *network* that contains them. As responsive designers, we need to focus not just on the individual bits of a design, but also the relationship between those elements within a larger layout system. Joe Stewart described the responsive redesign of Virgin America in similar terms—not focused exclusively on individual breakpoints, but with a wider, more holistic view (http://bkaprt.com/rdpp/05-02/):

> For whatever reason, people think it's okay to have focused user experiences being on mobile, but when you get to desktop it's about throwing in the kitchen sink. One of the great things about responsive is that it forces you to make those mobile decisions on a desktop...In terms of the overall way to think about design and design process or responsive, some people like to say there's a mobile-first way of looking at things but with responsive it's everything first.

Tito Bottita, partner at design agency Upstatement, said that while "mobile first" is a critically important guiding principle, they planned the layout of the *Boston Globe* in a slightly different manner (http://bkaprt.com/rdpp/05-03/):

> Our designs began at 960px, arguably the most complicated breakpoint, with several columns of content. Maybe this just came naturally after years of designing for that width. But I think it's more than that. It's easier to design with more screen real-estate—you see more at one time, you have a more nuanced hierarchy...So starting at 960, we designed downward. Every decision informed the one before it and the one after; we flipped back and forth between breakpoints a lot. As the Mobile First mantra suggests, designing for mobile was most instructive because it forced us to decide what was most important. And since we refused to hide content between breakpoints,

the mobile view could send us flying back up to the top level to remove complexity. The process felt a bit like sculpting.

As Upstatement found, beginning from the widest, most complex layout didn't preclude them from refining the smallest view of the design—in many instances, reviewing the work at one breakpoint informed the shape of the other. You could use InDesign, as Upstatement did, to quickly create breakpoint-friendly designs, and balance them against each other. Or you could dive into HTML and CSS and create a responsive prototype. The tools are secondary, as there's a larger question at hand: how do we assemble all these distinct components into a larger, useful responsive design?

On that note, we should probably talk about the F-word.

FRAMEWORKS

A number of responsive-specific CSS frameworks have appeared in recent years. Bootstrap (http://bkaprt.com/rdpp/05-04/) and Foundation (http://bkaprt.com/rdpp/05-05/) are two of the most popular, allowing you to quickly create responsive layouts using their established markup (**FIG 5.1**). For example, here's how to create a three-column row of elements with Foundation:

```
<div class="row">
  <div class="small-4 columns">...</div>
  <div class="small-4 columns">...</div>
  <div class="small-4 columns">...</div>
</div>
```

By default, Foundation's layouts are built on a twelve-column grid. By using small-4, a class that describes the number of columns each element should span, Foundation's CSS will arrange our three elements in each row (**FIG 5.2–5.3**). And if we wanted to change the priority at a wider breakpoint, we simply need to describe that change in the markup:

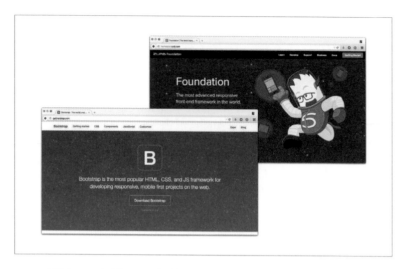

FIG 5.1: Third-party CSS frameworks, like Bootstrap and Foundation, can help you build a responsive layout more quickly.

```
<div class="row">
  <div class="small-12 medium-3 columns">...</div>
  <div class="small-12 medium-6 columns">...</div>
  <div class="small-12 medium-3 columns">...</div>
</div>
```

Above a specific breakpoint—in Foundation, that defaults to a viewport width above 650px—our medium- classes allow the middle div to span six columns, while the outer divs are reduced to three columns each. And that's all made possible by simply changing a few classes in our HTML.

Neat, right? I think CSS frameworks, responsive or otherwise, are fantastic. If you're working in a team environment, a CSS framework—whether off-the-shelf or developed internally—can take a lot of subjectivity out of creating layouts, eliminate arbitrary class names and HTML structures, and ensure all collaborators are using the same conventions. And for prototyping, there's nothing better: when I'm discussing

FIG 5.2: A row of three elements, built from simple markup on the Foundation framework.

FIG 5.3: With a few of Foundation's markup patterns, we've got a flexible, responsive grid layout.

responsive designs with a client, I'll often grab a third-party CSS framework to quickly mock up a page, using disposable code to get a layout into browsers as quickly as possible. But most important, these third-party CSS frameworks are wonderful

	BOOTSTRAP	FOUNDATION
Small screens	Below 768px	Below 640px
Medium screens	Above 768px	Above 641px
Large screens	Above 992px	Above 1024px
Extra large screens	Above 1200px	Above 1440px

FIG 5.4: Bootstrap and Foundation, two popular responsive frameworks, define their breakpoints in pixels, using values that are closely aligned with common device sizes.

learning resources, allowing designers to better understand the fundamentals of page layout.

But they're heavy.

When I say "heavy," I'm not referring to the weight of the code used in the frameworks, though that could be a valid concern; their additional classes and markup can be, well, bulky. And as we'll see later in the chapter, many CSS-based methods allow us to create robust layout systems without describing columns and rows in our markup.

But putting the bytes aside, there's a larger concern: CSS frameworks are *conceptually* heavy. The layouts they provide are bound to an ideal grid, usually with twelve or sixteen columns of uniform widths. From there, the classes in the markup describe how that grid should adapt at specific breakpoints. And when it comes to Foundation and Bootstrap, the breakpoints they use are very device-specific (FIG 5.4).

It's worth noting that these are default values, and they're easy to change. But the out-of-the-box breakpoints are closely associated with specific common devices: 768px is a common width for 10" tablets, like the iPad, held in portrait mode; 640px lines up with many smartphones, like the Samsung Galaxy or HTC One, in landscape mode.

As extensible and well-engineered as these frameworks are, their breakpoints are a snapshot of the web as we currently understand it. With the increasing proliferation of browsers, screen sizes, and device classes, we need lighter frameworks—

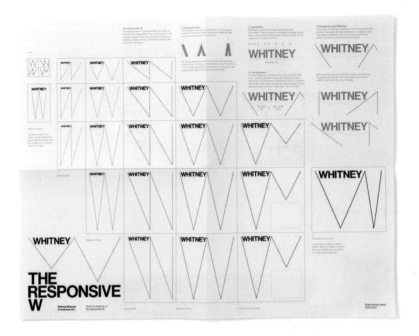

FIG 5.5: The Whitney's new logo in action, which they (coincidentally!) call their "responsive W" (http://bkaprt.com/rdpp/05-07/).

frameworks that can adapt as nimbly as our designs themselves, ensuring they survive beyond just "mobile, tablet, and desktop."

IN 2013, THE WHITNEY MUSEUM rebranded, launching an elegant site (http://bkaprt.com/rdpp/05-06/) alongside its new identity (FIG 5.5). Both are cool, contemporary affairs, emphasizing expansive margins and bold, angular lines. While the logo may seem spare and minimal, it has a dizzying array of applications. It can incorporate artwork from the museum, and even be encountered on differently shaped media throughout museumgoers' days (FIG 5.6-7). On the Whitney's semi-responsive website, the logo changes dramatically at different breakpoints. Yet among all these variations across countless kinds of media, as much as it reshapes itself, the mark is still recognizable as the Whitney's distinctive "W" (FIG 5.8).

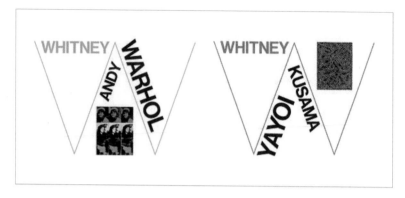

FIG 5.6: As flexible as it is minimal, the Whitney's logo can incorporate artwork from the museum (http://bkaprt.com/rdpp/05-07/).

FIG 5.7: The logo also lives in the physical world, sketched here as it might appear on a bus shelter (http://bkaprt.com/rdpp/05-07/).

FIG 5.8: The Whitney's logo is just as adaptive as their website, wonderfully enough.

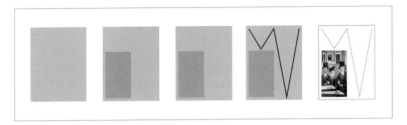

FIG 5.9: A simple framework can yield hundreds, if not thousands, of logo variations (http://bkaprt.com/rdpp/05-07/).

Now, you'd be forgiven for thinking that across all these hundreds, if not thousands, of variations that there was some massive computer churning away in a closet, with pillars of smoke pouring out as it generated algorithmically perfect variations of the logo. (Okay, the secret's out: I've never actually seen a computer.) But no! As it happens, the designers of the logo came up with a straightforward technique for generating a near-infinite number of adaptations (**FIG 5.9**):

1. Within a specific area—a piece of paper or a section of a web page—there will be some elements that need to be incorporated.
2. Divide the remaining available area into four equal columns.
3. From there, it's a simple matter of connecting the dots: from the top of the first column to the bottom of the next; the bottom of the second column to the top of the third; and so on until the "W" is complete (**FIG. 5.9**).

This is, in every sense of the word, a *framework,* but it's so much lighter than the ones we use on the web. It's focused less on *execution*—on laying out specific elements or arranging the columns and rows—and more on defining the characteristics of a desirable outcome: of shaping the conditions that would give rise to a successful mark. And with all the challenges we're facing—and those we're about to face—this is a wonderful model for the kinds of frameworks we *really* need on the web.

THERE'S A STORY that might be relevant here. It's a story about two artists, a boy who dreamed, and drawings that moved.

In the early part of the twentieth century, cartoonist Winsor McCay was one of the most widely circulated artists in the United States. His masterpiece, *Little Nemo in Slumberland,* was massively popular, and with good reason: his broadsheet-sized comics were awash with color and detail, featuring cinematic layouts that have been all but lost on modern newspapers' ever-shrinking comics pages (**FIG 5.10**).

Reportedly inspired by his son's flip books, McCay decided to try his hand at "making moving pictures." His first attempt required over four thousand frames, each meticulously hand-drawn, and featured the characters of *Little Nemo* dancing, fighting, and smoking the odd cigar. (**FIG 5.11**) Over the next decade, McKay created ten films, showcasing his characteristic style and draftsmanship, and translating his lovingly hatched line art into motion. And they are, each and every one of them, stunning (**FIG 5.12**).

I don't think it diminishes any of McCay's achievements to suggest that his animation also feels, well, a tad rudimentary. Viewed through modern eyes, it's easy to see where footage is reused or reversed, allowing McCay to conserve a little effort, and his characters' movements are often a bit mechanical. That's not a criticism—working alongside early animators like Émile Cohl, James Stuart Blackton, and Max Fleischer, McCay and his peers were at the forefront of defining what animation could be.

But it wasn't until Walt Disney formed his studio a few decades later that people began to take animation seriously as an art form. That might sound a bit strong, but it's true: the

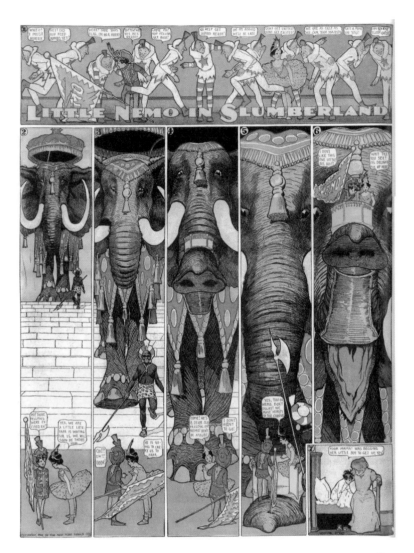

FIG 5.10: Winsor McKay's *Little Nemo in Slumberland* is stunning, even over a century after its publication. And thankfully, it's freely available on the Internet Archive (http://bkaprt. com/rdpp/05-08/).

FIG 5.11: For his first animated short film, Winsor McKay adapted *Little Nemo* for the screen. Video image from YouTube (http://bkaprt.com/rdpp/05-09/).

FIG 5.12: McKay's handcrafted films were part of the earliest days of line-drawn animation, covering topics ranging from the slightly macabre (http://bkaprt.com/rdpp/05-10/), to the patently adorable (http://bkaprt.com/rdpp/05-11/), to the sweepingly dramatic *The Sinking of the Lusitania* (http://bkaprt.com/rdpp/05-12/).

characters in Disney's features possessed an elegance of motion that hadn't been seen in animated movies before. Marc Davis, one of the studio's original animators, said that when Walt Disney started his studio, "animation had been done before, but stories were never told." Now, that is some forceful trash-talking, as Davis is calling out everyone who'd ever tried their hand at animation before Disney—but I think there's some truth to it. To be honest, it's pretty hard to exaggerate the effect the studio's work had on filmgoing audiences. Once those simple, spare line drawings were colored and animated, they felt real. They felt *human*. And that's something that hadn't really been done before.

The studio's success was due, in part, to Disney himself, but it wasn't because he was a more talented animator than his employees or competitors. Rather, it was because he was an incredibly exacting director; he demanded that the animation his studio produced possess a "caricature of realism" or "illusion of life" with which his audiences could connect and empathize. Some decades later, two of Disney's original animators, Frank Thomas and Ollie Johnston, borrowed that phrase as the title of their wonderful book, *The Illusion of Life*. In it, Thomas and Johnston define what they called "The Twelve Basic Principles of Animation," which allowed Disney's animators to meet Walt's rather exacting demands. These principles—covering animation concepts like staging, timing, arcs, and more—were the bedrock for the studio's work, and have become the foundation for what we consider to be quality animation in modern times (**FIG 5.13**).

On a personal note, I can't recommend Thomas and Johnston's book highly enough—it's a lovely read, especially for such a technical book. But if you're pressed for time, a paraphrased version of their guidelines are available on their website (http://bkaprt.com/rdpp/05-15/). As you read through them, you'll notice these principles aren't especially technical. Rather than using obtuse jargon, they explain *how* to judge whether or not a drawing possesses that illusion of life that defined Disney's work. Did a character's arm properly "anticipate" that it was about to throw a ball? Did a character's gait have enough "squash and stretch" as it walked from one end of the frame to the other?

These principles were a kind of a shared vocabulary, one that allowed the studio's animators to discuss how their work measured up to Disney's famously high standards. Rather than dictating the use of certain animation techniques or emphasiz-

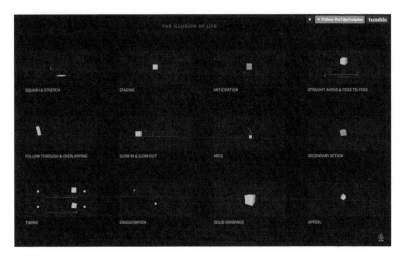

FIG 5.13: Disney's principles of animation were recently adapted by Cento Lodigiani into—you guessed it—an animated primer that demonstrates them handily (http://bkaprt.com/rdpp/05-13/). Video image from Tumblr (http://bkaprt.com/rdpp/05-14/).

ing steps in their production workflow, the principles allowed the studio to discuss and evaluate the *quality* of its work.

This is the conversation we need to have.

Over the past few years, we've been learning how to adapt our layouts to the infinite canvas of the web. Our sites can be viewed on any size screen, at any time, and responsive design is one approach that lets us accommodate the web's variable shape. But with all of the challenges we're facing and those yet to come, we need to begin building not just patterns, but *principles* for responsive design—principles that will allow us to focus not just on layout, but on the quality of our work.

If each part of your responsive interface is more or less self-contained—with its own layout rules, content needs, and breakpoints—then the code behind each element's design is far less important than thinking carefully about *how* and *why* an element should adapt. In other words, how do we move beyond thinking in terms of columns and rows, and start talking about the quality of our responsive designs? And what would frameworks to support that look like?

FINDING THE WORDS

Honestly, there's no perfect answer to that question. But recently, a number of designers and organizations have started sharing the vocabulary they use to decide how and when their responsive designs should adapt. Vox Media, for example, thinks of their content as existing within a river—and in keeping with the metaphor, the flow of that content can be interrupted at certain points. Here's how they describe the front pages of Vox.com (http://bkaprt.com/rdpp/05-16/):

> Content flows around "rocks" and "breakers", which are modules such as a "Most Commented" list or a row of "Popular Videos." Many of these behaviors remain in the new layout system, but the key difference is an added contextual layer. Elements in the river are laid out to better highlight the diversity of content on Vox — articles, features, videos, editorial apps, card stacks, to name a few. Each one displays differently depending on its type and neighboring entries.

Note that the language they use to talk about the quality of their layouts doesn't revolve around columns or rows. There's nary a mention of grids. For Vox, the design process begins with content priority and evolves into a layout. By understanding the weight and importance of each piece of content that flows through the river, the Vox team can algorithmically generate a responsive layout that best reflects the importance of the information within it.

Starting with an abstract system of columns and rows would be wrong for them—and, I'd argue, for every web designer. After all, according to Mark Boulton, there are three fundamental benefits of a grid system (http://bkaprt.com/rdpp/05-17/):

- Grid systems **create connectedness.** A well-made grid can visually connect related pieces of content or, just as importantly, separate unrelated elements from each other. In other words, they help us create narratives from our layout.
- By establishing predefined alignment points, grid systems help designers **solve layout problems.**

- *A well-designed grid system will **provide visual pathways for the reader's eye to follow**, and allow them to better understand a visual hierarchy.*

As Boulton notes, we historically created grid systems by adopting a "canvas in" method. Working from the edges of a printed page, designers would subdivide a page into a system of columns and rows, and place images and text upon that grid in pleasing, rational arrangements. But the web doesn't have any such boundary—after all, it's the first truly fluid design medium. As a result, Boulton argues we should instead adopt a "content out" approach to designing our grids: to build more complex layout systems out from a foundation of small, modular pieces of content. And to do so, Boulton proposes three guiding principles:

- ***Define relationships from your content.*** *A grid for the web should be defined by the content, not the edge of an imaginary page.*
- ***Use ratios or relational measurements above fixed measurements.***
- ***Bind the content to the device.*** *Use CSS media queries, and techniques such as responsive web design, to create layouts that respond to the viewport.*

By understanding the shape of our content, we can create flexible layouts that support connectedness—not just between related pieces of information, but between our layouts and the device. We can make responsive grid systems that don't just fit on an ever-increasing number of screens—they'll feel at home, wherever they're viewed.

FINDING THE SEAMS

Principles are wonderful, of course, but we still have to find a means of implementing them: of translating those ideals into practical responsive patterns and layouts. For me, that "content out" process begins by looking at the smallest version of a piece of content, then expanding that element until its seams begin to show and it starts to lose its shape. Once that happens, that's an opportunity to make a change—to introduce a breakpoint that reshapes the element and preserves its integrity.

But first, we need a method of finding an element's seams, and understanding how it loses its shape. For me, that process begins by looking at four characteristics: **width**, **hierarchy**, **interaction**, and **density**.

Width

Width might be a little self-evident. As the width of a viewport changes, so does the width of a responsive design. But as the design gets wider or narrower, so will the elements within it, and as those modules expand or contract, there may be opportunities to add a breakpoint (**FIG 5.14**).

Hierarchy

Width is, I'm sure you'll agree, the most common characteristic of a responsive design—but it's not the only one. As the shape of an element changes, the *hierarchy* of elements may need to change as well.

Let's take a quick look at a product page on Tattly's responsive ecommerce site (http://bkaprt.com/rdpp/05-19/). When viewed on wider screens, the primary content area has two key pieces of information: a photo carousel of the product on the left, and a call to action to purchase the product on the right (**FIG 5.15**). But that's just one view of this particular part of the design, because as screens get narrower, we lose the ability to place multiple columns side by side. That's where a question of hierarchy arises: in a single-column layout, which piece of content should appear first? Tattly opted, quite rightly, to lead with photos of the product—but you may answer hierarchy questions differently on your site (**FIG 5.16**).

Hierarchy is generally a reminder to be more *vertically aware* in our designs. After all, we have `min-width` and `max-width` media queries, but can also avail ourselves of `min-height` and `max-height` queries more often. I think the navigation menu for

FIG 5.14: On her stunning responsive portfolio, Meagan Fisher adjusts the typography of certain elements—not just their layout—as their width expands and contracts (http://bkaprt.com/rdpp/05-18/).

FIG 5.15: On Tattly's responsive ecommerce site, the product content is laid out in a pleasing two-column grid on wider screens.

FIG 5.16: On narrower viewports, the hierarchy of product information shifts from two columns to one.

the Field Museum (http://bkaprt.com/rdpp/05-20/) beautifully balances vertical and horizontal layouts (**FIG 5.17**). On wider screens, the navigation is anchored to the left edge of the design, and spans the full height of the viewport. You may notice that they're using the flexible box model, or *flexbox*, an advanced CSS layout method we'll look at later in this chapter (http://bkaprt.com/rdpp/05-21/). But since flexbox allows elements to automatically fill the space available to them, as the menu gets taller or shorter, the navigation elements resize vertically—but below a certain width *or* height, the menu is placed at the top of the page.

By minding the navigation's vertical edges, the Field Museum was able to introduce alternate layouts to ensure the content inside their navigation menu was never concealed, obscured, or clipped. In other words, the breakpoints we introduce to our responsive designs aren't tied to the shape of a device's screen.

FIG 5.17: The responsive navigation for the Field Museum, which occupies the height of the design. Below a certain width, it moves to the top of the screen to avoid cropping.

Instead, our media queries defend the integrity of the content we're designing.

Interaction

The way we *interact* with an element may change along with the design. Responsive navigation systems are probably the most obvious example of this. As we saw in Chapter 2, menus are often displayed in full at wider breakpoints but concealed at smaller ones, perhaps hidden behind expandable icons or links when space is at a premium (**FIG 5.18**).

But navigation isn't the only kind of content that might require interaction changes. For example, take the responsive sports brackets designed by SB Nation (http://bkaprt.com/rdpp/05-23/). While they appear as complex-looking charts at wider breakpoints, a simpler, more linear view of the brackets is shown on smaller screens (**FIG 5.19**). Along with the simplified layout, the brackets are presented as carousels in the smaller view, where real estate is more dear. Each of the four regions for the bracket are a single slide in the carousel, allowing the user to cycle through for details. The information in both visual states is the same, but the interaction model changes.

FIG 5.18: Karen McGrane's company site has a traditional-looking navigation at wider breakpoints, but on smaller viewports the user toggles the visibility of the menu. Same links, but a new interaction model (http://bkaprt.com/rdpp/05-22/).

Density

Finally, the amount of information you're showing in an element might need to vary over time—in other words, the *density* of information can change. The *Guardian*'s feature on the 2015 Oscars is full of examples of this, with responsively designed timelines displaying a significant amount of movie data. Above a

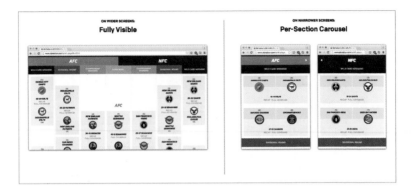

FIG 5.19: I don't know from sports, but I know I like SB Nation's responsive brackets: complex charts on wide screens, but a carousel of match-ups on smaller viewports. Same information, different interaction.

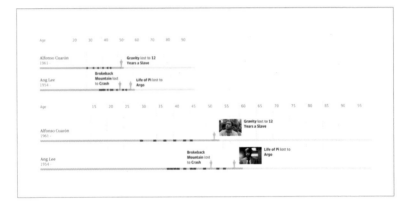

FIG 5.20: The *Guardian*'s responsive cinematic timelines gradually increase in density, displaying an extra image above a certain width (http://bkaprt.com/rdpp/05-24/).

certain width, thumbnail images are loaded in, slightly increasing the visual (and informational) density of the timeline (**FIG 5.20**).

Density is, as you might have guessed, an area where you should tread very carefully. As we've discussed before, remov-

FIG 5.21: Tattly hides its submenu entirely, reducing its navigation to a list of primary sections on smaller screens.

ing or hiding information because it doesn't fit can be problematic (**FIG 5.21**). Personally, I think the *Guardian*'s timelines work so well because the images shown at wider breakpoints are enhancements: they're not critical to understanding the information around them. Could they have designed alternate versions of the timelines to show images at all breakpoints? Possibly. But I think this is a wonderful example of density used to lighten the visual impact of a design, removing extraneous information without impeding access to the content.

SHAPING OUR SEAMS: MOVING BEYOND CLASSES

Width, hierarchy, interaction, and density work incredibly well for identifying the outer limits of our tiny layout systems, but you may want to supplement them with other concepts. Recently, designer Nathan Ford suggested a number of useful patterns for identifying when *relationships* between elements begin to break down, including layout anti-patterns like sevens,

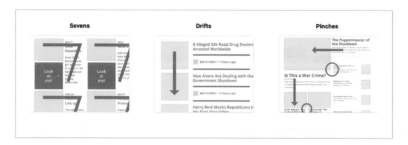

Sevens	Drifts	Pinches

FIG 5.22: Sevens, drifts, and pinches—oh my! Nathan Ford suggests a number of useful areas where your design might degrade (http://bkaprt.com/rdpp/05-25/).

FIG 5.23: Editorially's responsive dashboard used a custom, lightweight framework to create content-driven breakpoints.

drifts, and pinches (**FIG 5.22**). But regardless of how you choose to find the seams in your layout, moving beyond simple markup classes will give you considerably more flexibility.

Editorially, a (sadly defunct) web service for writers and editors I cofounded, used a custom layout framework for the

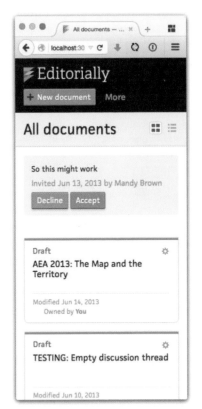

FIG 5.24: The foundation for Editorially's layout? A single-column grid.

most complex parts of its interface. The most visible example of this was on Editorially's dashboard, which displayed a list of documents owned by and shared with the user (FIG 5.23). As part of the team that built the dashboard, I started with a small-screen-friendly layout: a series of tasks and content, laid out vertically in a single-column, hierarchical grid (FIG 5.24).

Using a "mobile-friendly" layout as your foundation is a sign of a responsibly made responsive layout—but we don't have to stop at one column. For example, as Editorially's dashboard reached a width of 31em, it shifted to a two-column layout, using some concise CSS (FIG 5.25):

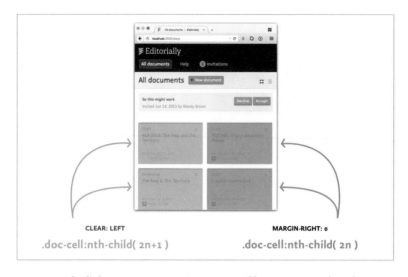

CLEAR: LEFT   MARGIN-RIGHT: 0
.doc-cell:nth-child(2n+1)   .doc-cell:nth-child(2n)

FIG 5.25: With a little `:nth-child()` magic, we can quickly create a two-column layout.

```
@media screen and (min-width: 31em) {
  /* Set widths */
  .doc-cell {
    float: left;
    width: 47.602739726027397260%;
      /* 278px / 584px */
  }
  /* Build the new layout */
  .doc-cell:nth-child(2n) {
    margin-right: 0;
  }
  .doc-cell:nth-child(2n+1) {
    clear: left;
  }
}
```

Wait—what just happened? Three selectors, and we have a new grid layout? Yep, and it's all thanks to the `:nth-child()` pseudo-class. Instead of relying on a CSS framework that requires classes in our HTML to describe our layout,

`:nth-child()` provides us with an incredibly powerful way to address specific elements of our design based on where they fall within the structure of our document. For example, if I wrote `.doc-cell:nth-child(4)`, my CSS would select the `.doc-cell` element that was the fourth child of its parent:

```
<div class="doc-grid">
  <div class="doc-cell">…</div>
  <div class="doc-cell">…</div>
  <div class="doc-cell">…</div>
  <div class="doc-cell">…</div>
  <div class="doc-cell">…</div>
</div>
```

Similarly, if I wrote `.doc-cell:nth-child(2)`, my rule would select the `.doc-cell` element that's the second child of our grid:

```
<div class="doc-grid">
  <div class="doc-cell">…</div>
  <div class="doc-cell">…</div>
  <div class="doc-cell">…</div>
  <div class="doc-cell">…</div>
  <div class="doc-cell">…</div>
</div>
```

Seems fairly straightforward, right? Well, things get *really* interesting when n appears inside `:nth-child()`. When that happens, n acts as a counter: its value begins at zero, then increments by one each time. So `:nth-child(2n)` becomes simple multiplication: just multiply the value of n by the number next to it, then add one to n, and then repeat the process.

```
2 × 0 = 0
2 × 1 = 2
2 × 2 = 4
2 × 3 = 6
…
```

In our CSS above, `.doc-cell:nth-child(2n)` is a way to instantly select every even-numbered cell in our grid, regardless of whether there are twenty cells in the grid, or twenty thousand. Once we've made that selection, applying a `margin-right: 0;` ensures that every second cell of our two-column grid is aligned flush against the right edge of the design.

`.doc-cell:nth-child(2n+1)`, on the other hand, selects every second cell—but the `+1` in the selector says we should start from *one,* not zero. Here's how the math would look:

```
(2 × 0) + 1 = 1
(2 × 1) + 1 = 3
(2 × 2) + 1 = 5
(2 × 3) + 1 = 7
...
```

Therefore, `.doc-cell:nth-child(2n+1)` applies a `clear: left` to every odd-numbered cell, ensuring that each row is a nice, discrete grouping of two documents (**FIG 5.25**).

Since we're using `:nth-child()`, rather than specific classes that exist in our markup, we can quickly—and dramatically—revise the grid's layout at each breakpoint. For example, as the dashboard viewport gets a little wider, we can introduce a three-column layout at a breakpoint of 44em (**FIG 5.26**):

```
/* 3-column */
@media screen and (min-width: 44em) {
  /* Set new widths */
  .doc-cell,
  .doc-cell:nth-child(n) {
    margin-right: 3.043968432919954904%;  /* 27 /
887 (per comp) */
    width: 31.003382187147688838%;
      /* 278px / 887px (per comp) */
  }
  /* Reset clears from previous breakpoint */
  .doc-cell:nth-child(n) {
    clear: none;
  }
```

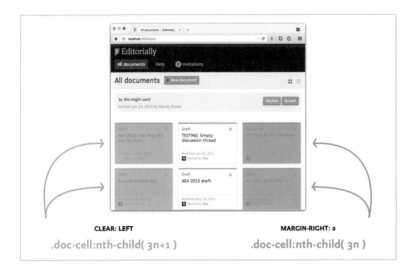

CLEAR: LEFT
.doc-cell:nth-child(3n+1)

MARGIN-RIGHT: 0
.doc-cell:nth-child(3n)

FIG 5.26: Another breakpoint, another grid layout: this time, three columns with :nth-child(3n).

```
/* Build the new layout */
.doc-cell:nth-child(3n) {
  margin-right: 0;
}
.doc-cell:nth-child(3n+1) {
  clear: left;
}
}
```

While this media query looks a little complex, it's simply repeating the process from our two-column layout:

1. New, flexible widths and margins are assigned to the doc-cell elements in our grid.
2. We can use :nth-child(n) to quickly reset styles inherited from the previous breakpoint. (In this case, we're removing the clear: left; applied to the start of each row.)
3. Then, we use :nth-child(3n) to remove the right margin of every third cell of our dashboard.

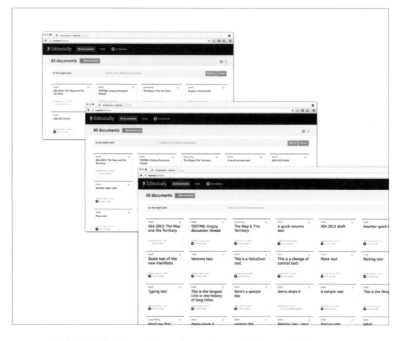

FIG 5.27: Sky's the limit: lightweight markup and powerful CSS can bring our responsive grids from four columns, to five, and finally up to a six-column layout. (And theoretically, beyond.)

4. Finally, `:nth-child(3n+1)` instructs the first cell in every three-column row to clear the cells before it.

I think you can see where this is going. Over time, Editorially's dashboard evolved from a single-column grid into two- and three-column variants, continuing all the way up to a final six-column layout (**FIG 5.27**). Realistically, we were only constrained by the time and resources we poured into the design. By moving the layout logic out of markup and into CSS, we gained infinitely more flexibility (**FIG 5.28**).

Thankfully, it's not just `:nth-child()`. There are a *truckload* of equally nimble layout tools coming out of the CSS specification. Flexbox, which places elements in horizontal or vertical

FIG 5.28: Index pages on our site for the Responsive Design Podcast use a similar :nth-child()-based layout framework (http://bkaprt.com/rdpp/05-26/).

stacks, is one of the most popular. The masthead on Frank Chimero's blog is a wonderful example of this. By setting display: flex on the header, the two elements within it—the navigation and his logo—are immediately laid out horizontally, each becoming a column occupying the full width that row (**FIG 5.29**).

Hypothetically, if Chimero were so inclined, he could reverse the order of the two elements by adding flex-direction: row-reverse to the masthead—all without touching the markup (**FIG 5.30**). This acts a bit like a change in gravity: while they're still laid out in a row, the order of the two items instantly reverses.

These more lightweight layout models have become incredibly popular, and have been embraced by a number of responsive designs (**FIG 5.31**). But as flexible as they are, flexbox and :nth-child() aren't without their drawbacks. As Jake Archibald notes, flexbox is ideal for small-scale layouts, but can negatively affect page rendering if used for page-level grids (http://bkaprt.com/rdpp/05-30/). Additionally, some of these properties won't work in older browsers—:nth-child() isn't supported by Internet Explorer 8 or below, and display: flex won't work at all in IE9 or lower. (And confusingly, there are differing implementations of flexbox in IE10, Safari, and many versions of Android.)

But if we take these considerations to heart, and if we design appropriate fallbacks for the browsers that need them, these lightweight layout tools allow us to design grid systems that

FIG 5.29: Frank Chimero's lovely responsive site features a little flexbox in its layout (http://bkaprt.com/rdpp/02-27/).

FIG 5.30: By changing the flex-direction on a flexible box, you can quickly reverse the, um, direction of the elements within it.

are effectively infinite in scale. As we move away from device-specific breakpoints, and adapt our layout systems according to the location of their seams, we'll be creating more robust, more future-friendly layouts. In other words, we'll be better prepared for the devices and browsers we haven't even imagined yet.

FIG 5.31: Google Chrome's platform reference (http://bkaprt.com/rdpp/05-27/), the ConvergeSE conference (http://bkaprt.com/rdpp/05-28/), and the *Guardian* (http://bkaprt.com/rdpp/05-29/): all fine examples of flexbox lovingly applied to multi-device layouts.

THE SEAMS WITHIN

And really, that's the sticking point, isn't it? We've moved far beyond the desktop, but we're still trying to find the right words to encompass the scope of what we're designing and where it'll appear. Despite that shift, the three words I hear most often on a responsive project—"mobile," "tablet," and "desktop"— are also the least helpful. They're not *bad* as such, but they're shorthand and often obscure the design challenges we face.

As a quick example, ask a colleague to describe what "mobile" means to them. Depending on who you ask, the term might suggest a small, touchscreen-enabled device, one that uses a slower cellular network to browse the web. But what if the user's device is connected to Wi-Fi? Alternately, "desktop" might suggest a widescreen device, perhaps with a mouse or trackpad. But what if their laptop's tethered to their phone's 3G connection? What if it also has a touch interface?

In other words, it's not just that we're designing for more device classes than ever before. Rather, the lines between "mobile," "tablet," and "desktop" are blurring: there are phones approaching the size of some smaller tablets (and vice versa); our sites can appear on web-enabled smartwatches, with view-

FIG 5.32: Responsive on your wrist: GOV.UK's lovely responsive site, as rendered on a Moto 360 smartwatch. Screenshots courtesy Anna Debenham.

FIG 5.33: Don't Digg and drive, kids: Tesla's Model S electric car has a touchscreen that, yes, has a WebKit-based browser. Photograph by Chris Martin (http://bkaprt.com/rdpp/05-31/).

INPUT METHOD	Touch	Keyboard/ Mouse	Hybrid	Speech	Joystick/ Analog
SCREEN SIZE	Small	Mid-Range	Wide		
NETWORK SPEED	Slow (EDGE/ GPRS)	Medium (3G)	Fast		
NETWORK CONDITION	Primarily Offline	Spotty, high latency	Reliable, stable		

FIG 5.34: Rather than discussing broad device classes, it's helpful to focus on specific features and conditions that might affect your responsive design.

ports roughly the same size as many smartphones (**FIG. 5.32**); heck, there are cars available today with browsers embedded in their dashboards (**FIG. 5.33**).

These are just a few reasons why I find it helpful to talk about *features,* not device classes. For example, I'll often talk with clients about how a responsive design performs across a few broad categories, usually focusing on **input method, screen size, network speed,** and **network condition** (**FIG. 5.34**).

It's not a comprehensive list, of course: an animation-heavy project might need a row for the quality of various devices' graphics processors, or perhaps you'll want finer-grained options in the network rows. And my row of input methods is often too brief, almost to a fault—perhaps you're designing for gestural interfaces, directional pad-driven devices like TV remotes or console controllers, or stylus-enabled screens.

But a table *like* this helps me decouple discussions of layout and screen size from, say, the quality of the user's network, or the input method she uses to interact with her device. Doing so helps avoid situations where it's assumed that every widescreen device is mouse-enabled, or that every small device is limited to a spotty 3G connection.

Much of this book has been about breaking down the page into its component parts: understanding how our small layout systems need to adapt, and then using those modules to gradually build more complex, responsive layout systems. As our layouts become more flexible and device-agnostic, the words we use to talk about our responsive designs should follow suit. Because when we're accounting for the conditions under which our responsive designs might be viewed—the myriad network conditions, input modes, and screen sizes—we need a design language that's as nimble and modular as our layout systems are becoming.

After all, these challenges aren't new. In a sense, we've been walking through this forest for some time, and we've got quite some distance to go yet. But as we walk, it's worth remembering there will always be trees around us, and we'll still manage to build beautiful, nimble, responsive designs.

Let's get started.

RESOURCES

Responsive Pattern Libraries

If you'd like to learn more about organizations using pattern libraries in their responsive designs, the Responsive Web Design Podcast I co-host with Karen McGrane has a number of episodes that might interest you. The interviews with Marriott (http://bkaprt.com/rdpp/06-01/), Code for America (http://bkaprt.com/rdpp/06-02/), Capital One (http://bkaprt.com/rdpp/06-03/; http://bkaprt.com/rdpp/01-16/), Virgin America (http://bkaprt.com/rdpp/02-23/), and Ushahidi (http://bkaprt.com/rdpp/06-04/) are especially relevant.

If you're interested in the process of building a style guide or pattern library, Susan Robertson's "Creating Style Guides" (http://bkaprt.com/rdpp/06-05/) is a great primer. Additionally, Anna Debenham's book, *Front-end Style Guides,* is as well-written as it is brief, and provides a wonderful introduction to the hows and whys of creating a pattern library (http://bkaprt.com/rdpp/06-06/).

While we're speaking of All Things Debenham: alongside Brad Frost, Anna co-hosted the Style Guide Podcast, which looks at the technical, visual, and organizational challenges of designing and maintaining pattern libraries (http://bkaprt.com/rdpp/06-07/).

Responsive Images

Mat Marquis wrote the original article that kicked off the responsive images discussion, and is very much worth your time (http://bkaprt.com/rdpp/06-08/). If you're hoping to learn about the various parts of the responsive images specification, two articles in particular were invaluable to me: namely, Eric Portis' "Responsive Images in Practice" (http://bkaprt.com/rdpp/06-09/), and Yoav Weiss' "Native Responsive Images" (http://bkaprt.com/rdpp/06-10/).

And finally, Scott Jehl's wonderful *Responsible Responsive Design* covers picture, srcset, and sizes in great detail, but also discusses *why* they're so critical from a performance stand-point (http://bkaprt.com/rdpp/06-11/).

More Layout Modules

Given the short stature of this little book, there wasn't space enough to cover all the wonderful layout techniques available to us. The flexible box module, or "flexbox," was briefly covered in Chapter 5. To learn more, I recommend this brief, interactive tour (http://bkaprt.com/rdpp/06-12/), this overview from the Mozilla Developer Network (http://bkaprt.com/rdpp/06-13/), or this comprehensive reference at CSS Tricks (http://bkaprt.com/rdpp/06-14/).

As I mentioned in Chapter 5, flexbox is great for detail work, but less than ideal for page layouts. Thankfully, there's an entire CSS module for creating grid layouts called, *ahem,* CSS Grid Layout. The module's specification is dense, but worth reading (http://bkaprt.com/rdpp/06-15/). If you're as interested in CSS Grid Layout as I am, I strongly recommend Rachel Andrews' resources (http://bkaprt.com/rdpp/06-16/; http://bkaprt.com/rdpp/06-17/) on the topic, as well as her stellar collection of CSS Grid Layout examples (http://bkaprt.com/rdpp/06-18/).

General Interest

If you're interested to learn more about Pius "Mau" Piailug, who sailed oceans using only the sky, I recommend this page on his 1976 journey to Tahiti (http://bkaprt.com/rdpp/06-19/), or this Smithsonian profile of traditional navigators (http://bkaprt.com/rdpp/06-20/). Wikipedia also has a great overview of his star compass and how it works (http://bkaprt.com/rdpp/06-21/).

If you'd like to read more about Pando, the beautiful tree that opened this book, the web is filled with wonderful resources. Start with Atlas Obscura (http://bkaprt.com/rdpp/06-22/), and learn about Pando's slightly troubled future due to climate change-induced drought, disease, and pests at http://bkaprt.com/rdpp/06-23/.

ACKNOWLEDGEMENTS

As always, my sincere thanks to A Book Apart. Katel LeDû, Jeffrey Zeldman, and Jason Santa Maria are among the finest, most inspiring people I know. They've built a wonderful publishing house, and I'm honored this book is a small part of it.

I was excited about writing this book, sure: but I was *ecstatic* when Erin Kissane agreed to edit it. In addition to her work at OpenNews, Erin is one of the finest writers and editors I know. She's uniquely gifted at untangling even the most knotted phrase, and responds to the dumbest authorial questions with grace, patience, and wit. If you enjoyed this book, you're likely seeing her hand at work.

Many people know Mandy Brown for her writing, her striking designs, or her years of working with product companies and publishers. Fewer people know Mandy was responsible for helping responsive design find its audience. After hearing my first presentation on responsive design, she invited me to write the original article for A List Apart; a year or so later, she edited and published *Responsive Web Design,* my first solo book. That's why I'm beyond thrilled she agreed to write the foreword for this one.

I've had the honor of working with many technical editors, but Anna Debenham is among the finest. Her feedback was in equal parts brilliant, challenging, and insightful. The book is much, much better for her tireless work.

Livia Labate, Scott Jehl, Mat Marquis, and Karen McGrane provided feedback on early drafts. I'm indebted to each of them for their time, their feedback, and their friendship.

I first learned of Pando from a talk by Matthew Battles at a mini-conference organized by Deb Chachra. I'm indebted to both.

And finally, but most importantly, my most heartfelt thanks to my wife Elizabeth for her patience, support, and love. This book, and everything else, is for her.

REFERENCES

Shortened URLs are numbered sequentially; the related long URLs are listed below for reference.

Chapter 1

01-01 https://commons.wikimedia.org/wiki/File:FallPando02.jpg

01-02 http://www.nps.gov/brca/naturescience/quakingaspen.htm

01-03 http://www.jstor.org/stable/1312652

01-04 http://trentwalton.com/2012/02/02/redefined/

01-05 http://www.fieldmuseum.org/

01-06 http://www.audubon.org/

01-07 http://cooking.nytimes.com/guides/how-to-make-pie-crust

01-08 http://laphamsquarterly.org/

01-09 http://www.microsoft.com/

01-10 https://www.virginamerica.com/

01-11 http://www.adobe.com/

01-12 https://www.gov.uk/

01-13 https://playbook.cio.gov/

01-14 http://www.google.com/trends/2014/

01-15 http://abookapart.com/products/responsive-web-design

01-16 http://responsivewebdesign.com/podcast/capital-one-part-two.html

01-17 http://responsivewebdesign.com/podcast/virgin-america.html

01-18 http://ushahidi.github.io/platform-pattern-library/

01-19 http://ux.mailchimp.com/patterns

01-20 http://www.starbucks.com/static/reference/styleguide/

01-21 http://patterns.alistapart.com/

01-22 https://commons.wikimedia.org/wiki/File:HMS_Dauntless_D33.jpg

01-23 http://us5.campaign-archive2.com/?u=7e093c5cf4&id=ead8a72012&e=ecb25a3f93

01-24 http://www.cisco.com/c/en/us/solutions/collateral/service-provider/visual-networking-index-vni/white_paper_c11-520862.html

01-25 http://www.comscore.com/Insights/Blog/Is-Mobile-Bringing-About-the-Death-of-the-PC-Not-Exactly

01-26 http://www.pcmag.com/article2/0,2817,2375047,00.asp

01-27 http://ben-evans.com/benedictevans/2014/4/25/ipad-growth

01-28 http://recode.net/2014/07/30/exclusive-interview-best-buy-ceo-says-tablet-sales-are-crashing-sees-hope-for-pcs/

01-29   http://www.reuters.com/article/2014/11/14/us-google-glass-insight-idUSKCN0IY18E20141114

01-30   https://play.google.com/store/apps/details?id=com.appfour.wearbrowser

01-31   https://www.youtube.com/watch?v=sGo08-SP_Ww

01-32   http://www.digitaltrends.com/computing/windows-8-1-preview-review/

01-33   http://www.ofcom.org.uk/static/cmr-10/UKCM-4.13.html

01-34   https://www.flickr.com/photos/anna_debenham/19700844223

01-35   http://www.ericsson.com/res/docs/2014/ericsson-mobility-report-november-2014.pdf

01-36   https://www.flickr.com/photos/ericsson_images/15626948657/in/set-72157649326666221

Chapter 2

02-01   http://www.nlm.nih.gov/exhibition/avoyagetohealth/exhibition-legacy.html

02-02   http://happycog.com/

02-03   http://responsivenews.co.uk/post/18948466399/cutting-the-mustard

02-04   http://responsivenews.co.uk/post/50028612882/responsive-news-testing

02-05   https://github.com/filamentgroup/Overthrow/

02-06   http://www.lukew.com/ff/entry.asp?1514

02-07   https://web.archive.org/web/20130819090807/http://stephanierieger.com/a-plea-for-progressive-enhancement

02-08   https://github.com/filamentgroup/Ajax-Include-Pattern/

02-09   http://www.filamentgroup.com/lab/responsive-design-approach-for-navigation.html

02-10   https://developer.mozilla.org/en-US/Apps/Design/UI_layout_basics/Responsive_Navigation_Patterns

02-11   https://www.quora.com/Who-started-the-trend-of-using-the-hamburger-icon-%E2%98%B0-as-a-menu-button

02-12   http://www.bbc.com/news/magazine-31602745

02-13   https://raygun.io/blog/2014/07/making-svg-html-burger-button/

02-14   http://sarasoueidan.com/blog/navicon-transformicons/

02-15   http://time.com

02-16   http://exisweb.net/mobile-menu-abtest

02-17   http://thenextweb.com/dd/2014/04/08/ux-designers-side-drawer-navigation-costing-half-user-engagement/

02-18   http://blog.booking.com/hamburger-menu.html

02-19   http://blog.manbolo.com/2014/06/30/apple-on-hamburger-menus

02-20   http://www.lukew.com/ff/entry.asp?933

02-21 http://www.bbc.com/news

02-22 http://www.theguardian.com/help/insideguardian/2014/jul/11/-sp-navigating-the-guardian

02-23 http://responsivewebdesign.com/podcast/virgin-america.html

02-24 https://the-pastry-box-project.net/dan-mall/2012-september-12

02-25 http://blog.mailchimp.com/redesigning-mailchimps-app-navigation/

02-26 https://www.filamentgroup.com/

02-27 http://frankchimero.com/blog/

Chapter 3

03-01 http://the.hitchcock.zone/wiki/Alfred_Hitchcock_and_Fran%C3%A7ois_Truffaut_%28Aug/1962%29_-_Part_2

03-02 http://clagnut.com/blog/268/

03-03 http://www.bbc.com/news/business-33436021

03-04 http://unstoppablerobotninja.com/entry/hand-over-the-ring/

03-05 http://thisismadebyhand.com/

03-06 http://alistapart.com/article/creating-intrinsic-ratios-for-video

03-07 http://www.w3.org/TR/css3-box/#padding1

03-08 http://www.paulirish.com/2008/conditional-stylesheets-vs-css-hacks-answer-neither/

03-09 http://virb.com/

03-10 http://vox.com/

03-11 http://httparchive.org/interesting.php?a=All&l=Jul%201%202015

03-12 http://googlesystem.blogspot.com/2010/07/googles-stats-about-web.html

03-13 http://blog.cloudfour.com/how-apple-com-will-serve-retina-images-to-new-ipads/

03-14 https://w3c.github.io/netinfo/

03-15 https://youtube.com/watch?v=d5_6yHixpsQ

03-16 http://www.gq.com/

03-17 http://digiday.com/publishers/gq-com-cut-page-load-time-80-percent/

03-18 http://ricg.io/

03-19 https://html.spec.whatwg.org/multipage/embedded-content.html#attr-img-srcset

03-20 https://html.spec.whatwg.org/multipage/embedded-content.html#introduction-3:viewport-based-selection-2

03-21 https://status.modern.ie/imgsrcset

03-22 https://github.com/scottjehl/picturefill

03-23   http://www.vox.com/2014/12/29/7458807/paul-krugman-economist
03-24   http://engineering.columbia.edu/model-created-map-
        energy-use-nyc-buildings
03-25   http://www.lars-mueller-publishers.com/en/programme-entwerfen
03-26   http://needmoredesigns.com/blog/early-responsive-design/
03-27   https://flic.kr/p/s7maT2
03-28   https://github.com/adamdbradley/focal-point
03-29   https://www.shopify.com/

Chapter 4

04-01   http://depts.washington.edu/chinaciv/graph/tcommain.htm
04-02   http://www.teleactivities.com/advertising-history/
04-03   http://blogs.ubc.ca/etec540sept10/2010/11/29/the-evolution-of-
        advertising-from-papyrus-to-youtube/
04-04   http://espressocoffee.quora.com/Coffee-timeline-A-literary-record
04-05   http://www.web-books.com/Classics/ON/B0/B701/15MB701.html
04-06   https://commons.wikimedia.org/wiki/File:Times_1788.12.04.jpg
04-07   https://www.flickr.com/photos/nesster/5511185739/
04-08   https://www.flickr.com/photos/42072348@N00/3049739879/
04-09   https://www.flickr.com/photos/91591049@N00/16587189580/
04-10   https://www.flickr.com/photos/nesster/14959218130/
04-11   https://www.flickr.com/photos/nesster/4822903313/
04-12   http://www.iab.net/guidelines/508676/508767/displayguidelines
04-13   http://www.iab.net/guidelines/508676/508767/mobileguidelines
04-14   https://github.com/filamentgroup/AppendAround
04-15   http://product.voxmedia.com/2014/12/17/7405131/algorithmic-design-
        how-vox-picks-a-winning-layout-out-of-thousands
04-16   http://markboulton.co.uk/journal/responsive-advertising
04-17   http://rogerblack.com/blog/post/the_holy_grail_part_i
04-18   http://rogerblack.com/blog/post/the_holy_grail_part_2
04-19   https://www.thinkwithgoogle.com/research-studies/the-new-
        multi-screen-world-study.html
04-20   http://responsivewebdesign.com/podcast/vox.html
04-21   http://advertising.theguardian.com/gallery/
04-22   http://next.theguardian.com/blog/responsive-takeover/
04-23   http://htmlads.monotype.com/
04-24   https://support.google.com/adsense/answer/3543893

04-25   http://www.iab.net/iablog/2014/03/viewability-has-arrived-what-you-need-to-know-to-see-through-this-sea-change.html

04-26   http://www.thedrum.com/news/2014/02/25/mwc-advertisers-lag-behind-publishers-creating-responsive-design-experiences-says

Chapter 5

05-01   http://trentwalton.com/2012/02/02/redefined/

05-02   http://responsivewebdesign.com/podcast/virgin-america.html

05-03   http://upstatement.com/blog/2012/01/how-to-approach-a-responsive-design/

05-04   http://getbootstrap.com/

05-05   http://foundation.zurb.com/

05-06   http://whitney.org/

05-07   http://www.experimentaljetset.nl/archive/whitney-museum-identity

05-08   https://archive.org/details/LittleNemo1905-1914ByWinsorMccay

05-09   https://www.youtube.com/watch?v=I-9FIFDHjLg

05-10   https://www.youtube.com/watch?v=1uLWbuButIE

05-11   https://www.youtube.com/watch?v=lmVra1mW7LU

05-12   https://www.youtube.com/watch?v=ws5kGs_J-CM

05-13   https://vimeo.com/93206523

05-14   http://the12principles.tumblr.com/

05-15   http://www.frankanollie.com/PhysicalAnimation.html

05-16   http://product.voxmedia.com/2014/12/17/7405131/algorithmic-design-how-vox-picks-a-winning-layout-out-of-thousands

05-17   http://www.markboulton.co.uk/journal/anewcanon

05-18   http://owltastic.com/

05-19   http://tattly.com/products/burger

05-20   http://www.fieldmuseum.org/

05-21   https://developer.mozilla.org/en-US/docs/Web/CSS/flex

05-22   http://www.bondartscience.com

05-23   http://www.sbnation.com/a/march-madness-2014

05-24   http://alistapart.com/article/content-out-layout

05-25   http://www.theguardian.com/film/ng-interactive/2015/feb/20/what-it-really-means-to-win-the-oscars-best-director

05-26   http://responsivewebdesign.com/podcast/

05-27   https://developer.chrome.com/home/platform-pillar

05-28   http://convergese.com/

05-29   http://www.theguardian.com/

05-30   http://jakearchibald.com/2014/dont-use-flexbox-for-page-layout/

05-31   https://www.flickr.com/photos/cjmartin/8916609941/

Resources

06-01   http://responsivewebdesign.com/podcast/marriott.html

06-02   http://responsivewebdesign.com/podcast/code-for-america.html

06-03   http://responsivewebdesign.com/podcast/capital-one.html

06-04   http://responsivewebdesign.com/podcast/ushahidi.html

06-05   http://alistapart.com/article/creating-style-guides

06-06   http://maban.co.uk/projects/front-end-style-guides/

06-07   http://styleguides.io/podcast/index.html

06-08   http://alistapart.com/article/responsive-images-how-they-almost-worked-and-what-we-need

06-09   http://alistapart.com/article/responsive-images-in-practice

06-10   https://dev.opera.com/articles/native-responsive-images/

06-11   http://www.abookapart.com/products/responsible-responsive-design

06-12   http://www.flexboxin5.com/

06-13   https://developer.mozilla.org/en-US/docs/Web/Guide/CSS/Flexible_boxes

06-14   https://css-tricks.com/snippets/css/a-guide-to-flexbox/

06-15   http://www.w3.org/TR/css3-grid-layout/

06-16   http://rachelandrew.co.uk/presentations/css-grid

06-17   http://rachelandrew.co.uk/archives/2014/06/27/css-grid-layout-getting-to-grips-with-the-chrome-implementation/

06-18   http://gridbyexample.com/

06-19   http://pvs.kcc.hawaii.edu/holokai/1976/ben_finney.html

06-20   http://www.smithsonianmag.com/smithsonian-institution/how-voyage-kon-tiki-misled-world-about-navigating-pacific-180952478/?no-ist

06-21   http://en.wikipedia.org/wiki/Mau_Piailug

06-22   http://www.atlasobscura.com/places/pando-the-trembling-giant

06-23   http://www.smithsonianmag.com/science-nature/whats-killing-the-aspen-93130832/?all

INDEX

A

Adobe 5
AdSense 111
AIDS.gov 5
Ajax-Include pattern 32, 99
A List Apart 10
AppendAround library 106
Apple 42
Archibald, Jake 74, 143
aspect ratio 62

B

Bale, Peter 112
BBC News 21, 45, 58
Beamly 41
Booking.com 41
Bootstrap 115
Boston Globe 31, 100, 114
Bottita, Tito 114
Boulton, Mark 108, 127
Bradley, Adam 83
breakpoint-sensitive ads 104
Brigleb, Raymond 83
Brundrett, Trei 109

C

Capital One 9
Childs, Scott 9
Chimero, Frank 55, 143
CNN International Digital 112
comps 52
conditional comments 68
conditional loading 99
conditionally loaded menus 29
CSS-based resizing 72

D

Davis, Marc 124
Disney animation studio 122
Disney.com 42
document.write() statements 102

E

Editorially 136
element hierarchy 129
embedded video 60
Ericsson 15

F

fallback styles 68, 143
Ferreira, Michel 41
Field Museum 4, 131
Filament Group 26, 32, 34, 106
Fisher, Meagan 130
Fishlake National Forest 1
FiveThirtyEight 29
flexbox 131, 142
flexible backgrounds 67
fluid videos 59
Ford, Nathan 135
Foster, James 40
Foundation 115
frameworks 115

G

Gerstner, Karl 83
Google 6, 111
GOV.UK 5, 146
Grigsby, Jason 72
Guardian 33, 47, 110, 133

H

hamburger icons 34
Happy Cog 18
Holgado, Federico 11
HotWired 94

I

information density 133
input methods 147
Interactive Advertising Bureau 93
iOS 42
Irish, Paul 68

J

JavaScript, testing for 20
Johnston, Ollie 125

K

Koblentz, Thierry 61

L

Lapham's Quarterly 4
Little Nemo in Slumberland 123
Lodigiani, Cento 126
low bandwidth 74

M

Made By Hand 60
MailChimp 10
Mall, Dan 52
McCay, Winsor 122
McGrane, Karen 133
Microsoft 5, 14
Monotype 111
Mozilla 34
MSNBC 26
Mulholland, Chris 47

N

National Audubon Society 4
navigation drawers 42
Network Information API 74
New York Times 4

O

Ofcom 15
off-canvas menus 28
O'Reilly 94
overflow (CSS property) 25
Overthrow.js library 26

P

Pando 2
Paravel 3
pattern libraries 10
percentage-based padding 64
Photoshop 52
Piailug, Pius "Mau" 16
progressive reveal 46
Publick Adviser 92

R

Responsive Issues Community Group
     74
Rutter, Richard 57

S

SB Nation 132
Shopify 85
Sketch 52
Smashing Magazine 95
srcset attribute 75
Starbucks 10
star compass 16
Stern, Mike 42
Stewart, Joe 9, 51, 114
Stocks, Elliott Jay 95
style guides 10

T

Tattly 129
Tesla 146
Thomas, Frank 125
Time magazine 35

U

Upstatement 114
US Digital Service 5
Ushahidi 10

V

Virb 69
Virgin America 5, 9, 51, 114
Vox 71, 106, 127

W

Walmart.ca 28
Walton, Trent 3, 113
Whitney Museum 119
Windows 8.1 14
Work & Co 51
wrist-based browsers 13
Wroblewski, Luke 44

X

Xerox Star 35

Y

Year in Search 2014 6
Young, Jesse 106

ABOUT A BOOK APART

We cover the emerging and essential topics in web design and development with style, clarity, and above all, brevity—because working designer-developers can't afford to waste time.

COLOPHON

The text is set in FF Yoga and its companion, FF Yoga Sans, both by Xavier Dupré. Headlines and cover are set in Titling Gothic by David Berlow.

This book was printed in the United States using FSC certified Finch papers.